WOMAN AT THE FRONT

WOMAN AT THE FRONT

Memoirs of an ATS Girl

D-Day to 1946

Sylvia Wild

AMBERLEY

This memoir is dedicated to my father who fought at Ypres in the First World War and was awarded The Military Medal. And to my two sons, David and Peter, and my two granddaughters, Katie and Hannah, all born after the Second World War and whose interest has greatly inspired me.

First published 2012

Amberley Publishing
The Hill, Stroud
Gloucestershire, GL5 4EP

www.amberleybooks.com

British Library Cataloguing in Publication Data.
A catalogue record for this book is available from the British Library.

ISBN 978 1 4456 0369 8

Typesetting and Origination by Amberley Publishing.
Printed in Great Britain.

Introduction

During the lifetimes of four women in my family, enormous changes were taking place in the roles they played, or were expected to play. First, there was my maternal grandmother, born in 1858, married when she was nineteen and who, by the time she died at the age of fifty-four, had raised thirteen children, all born at home and all survived – her whole life was devoted to her children and her husband. He was the breadwinner who had his own licensed Hackney cab (the forerunner of London's taxis).

Nan was their firstborn in 1878, a premature baby who lived to the age of seventy-eight. She married in 1906. She never had any children of her own; no doubt growing up with the almost annual arrival of a new baby in the family was not conducive to wanting any of her own. She certainly knew all about Marie Stopes, the pioneer of contraceptives, but I do not think she ever attended one of her clinics. Nan left school at thirteen years old, was literate, good at arithmetic and an avid reader. Her school lessons also included cookery, a must for all girls.

My mother, born in 1895, was the last but one of the thirteen siblings. She was sixteen when their mother died. As their father had died three or four years earlier, my aunt (Nan) and her husband took the four or five youngest children into their home. Without their selfless generosity those children would have been homeless. My mother married in 1920 and during the next ten years they had five children. In 1929 my father suffered redundancy. They lost their home and were in dire financial difficulties due to the Depression.

Once again, my aunt and uncle came to their rescue, and when I was seven and a half my older sister and I were taken in by them, leaving our younger sister and my two brothers with our parents.

And the last of the four generations of females was me, born in 1923 between the two World Wars. *Woman at the Front* is not intended to be an autobiography, but covers the first of my life's experiences, opening up a world which would have been entirely unknown to my grandmother, my elderly aunt and my mother.

A carefree existence before the war with my sister Joan (left).

Winter 1940. Still civilians working in London, where the bombing was very heavy.

1943. Both Joan (second from right) and I (left) were in the Army and had a quick change from our uniforms. Generous gifts of coupons provided us with very pretty dresses. A great rush over twenty-four hours.

Chapter 1

Having just returned from our doctor's surgery, where we eighty-year-olds sat with our walking sticks, wondering whether we would be able to get up again, the coughs and sneezes emanating from other patients took my mind back some sixty years.

It was the day General Montgomery, our Commanding Officer in HQ21 Army Group, had gathered together a small number of girls who had volunteered to serve abroad with HQ, some time after D-Day. The winter of 1943/44 was a bitterly cold one. I was billeted with two others in a flat at the top of Argyle Mansions in Hammersmith. The relentless nightly bombing, the lack of any heating or creature comforts was not much to go back to after long sessions taking dictation in shorthand and typing the transcriptions. In my own case this was invariably headed 'Top Secret – Operation Overlord'. But always there were cups of cocoa to revive me if I showed signs of flagging.

The noise of German bombers overhead would eventually be ignored as I laid my head on the pillows and sank into a deep sleep on a hard unrelenting wooden bed. If I had been working particularly hard I understood I would start talking in my sleep, and this kept the other two colleagues awake more than the bombing, but I never really believed them; nor did I believe what they related I had said.

To return to the small gathering with Montgomery; there we were, sitting in the small empty theatre in Hammersmith waiting for Monty, coughing and sneezing our heads off. He arrived and, eyeing this miserable audience, announced in his brusque manner that it was never his wish to take females abroad and, what was more, if there was one more cough or sneeze he would leave. We did our best.

When war broke out I was two months past my sixteenth birthday and into a two-year secretarial course. My subjects were Maths, Book-keeping, French, Higher English, Shorthand, Typing and Commerce (now called Economics). I did well in the last four, but French I was only beginning to grasp when I left, and Book-keeping and Maths were never my subjects.

Three days before war was declared my college was evacuated to Caversham, near Reading. I completed my final exams the following summer in 1940 and returned home to Clapham, south-west London, starting work as a shorthand typist in my sister's firm in Farringdon Street, off Fleet Street and Ludgate Hill. This was not ideal timing as in September the heavy bombing of London started, affecting us both at work and at home, involving difficult journeys and sleepless nights.

My sister Joan was called up into the ATS in 1942 and, after three months' additional training at Strathpeffer in Scotland, was posted into GHQ Home Forces, working in an office under Whitehall, Rotunda, where Churchill's war room was located. Early in 1943 I too was called up into the ATS. The initial experience of the three weeks' training, preparing one for army life was, for me, like falling into an abyss. First, our civilian clothes were packed into our suitcases ready to be sent home. Piled high with our army issue and wearing new unpressed uniforms and shoes that were the nearest they had to our actual size, we were shown to our quarters. These were Nissen huts containing about ten double bunks along either side; so we were sleeping around forty to a hut.

My particular intake (unfortunately for me) comprised mostly of north country mill girls. We were at High Legh between Knutsford and Warrington and I was from South London. Until then I had only heard of the North and South divide, and, oh boy, these girls had really lived. I was to learn a lot from them; in particular, one did not wait patiently for the use of the one and only iron. One would carefully draw away the attention of the next user and then seize it.

I chose an upper bunk not realising this was situated right next to a window that would be kept wide open all night. A hard mattress on wooden slats, with one unspeakable blanket underneath and one on top, was no place to experience a bitterly cold night and a morning call at 6.30 a.m. The ablutions were across a field situated in another Nissen hut; and of course there were more girls than sinks.

Our allocated Sergeant and Corporal gave us our first instructions. In the morning, before breakfast, we would all be assigned a cleaning duty. Mine was to wash, scrub and dry the step into our hut. I had never held a scrubbing brush in my life, but with my pail of water and soap I was ready for action on that first morning, only too anxious to leave my bunk after an almost sleepless night. These I was well used to after the experience of endless heavy bombing raids at home in London.

My clean step was ready for inspection by the Sergeant, only to be utterly ruined by the other girls returning their own equipment outside as instructed to do. So many feet crossing my clean step was not something I had envisaged. There was no time to do anything about it; we all stood to attention by the side of our bunks while the Sergeant ran her hands over anything that might be hiding some hidden dust. My step was left until last and I felt relieved that she hadn't noticed it; but of course I was to learn she missed nothing. As she was leaving she turned to report that breakfast was being served and all could leave except Private Cook, who would have to remain and carry out her duty again. Did I just imagine the relish with which she said this?

On that first morning, we had our inoculations. There was some flinching when these were carried out, but in this respect, we lived in an age when any protests were completely unacceptable, where our mothers were concerned. From babyhood you had to take your medicine, pricks in the arm, whatever, it was all for your own good. This session was followed by a lecture on army ranks, regulations, never to pass an officer without giving a smart salute and the expectation that we would work as a team. Without realising it, it was the daily square-bashing which brought this about. It developed a spirit of marching together, carrying out 'eyes right' together, 'left turn', 'right turn'. Unexpectedly, I found I quite enjoyed this daily parade and the team spirit it was developing, and yet I was still very much ME.

After three weeks we had our passing out parade and were inspected by the senior officer. The notice board contained our postings and I was dismayed to learn I was being posted out to a training unit for wireless operators. I made it known that I was a trained shorthand typist and that was where my ability should be used. I said my goodbyes to everyone and I was left behind.

Older sisters were able to 'claim' a younger one and I had not realised that my sister had been working on this, but as she was in GHQ in London, which was very 'hush-hush', my posting there would take longer. This meant I had to spend a short time in a holding unit at High Legh in Cheshire, where I was employed mainly peeling pounds and pounds of potatoes for the local Home Guard. This was organised (with relish I think) by the ATS officer in charge. When my posting to GHQ eventually came through, I had very blistered and sore hands. I could not make my move away fast enough.

Chapter 2

My introduction to GHQ Home Forces was not in London but in Virginia Water, Surrey, where they were having a brief respite from Hammersmith. I was taken to a large Nissen hut on the Wentworth Golf Course, where I would be working for the D. Tn (Director of Transportation) and his officers. At that time Brigadier Waghorn was D. Tn (Ports, Docks, Harbours and Railways). The hut was one of several below the clubhouse with about twenty-five Royal Engineers, one or two from the Royal Corps of Signals, presided over by a Regimental Sergeant Major and a Company Sergeant Major (RSM and CSM). The officers and draughtsmen were in other huts, dotted about on the green.

Initially there were only two females – an ATS clerk and me. I sat with my typewriter at one end. Due to the rounded roof, whispered conversations could be clearly heard relayed along the walls, as in the Whispering Gallery in St Paul's Cathedral, but newcomers had to discover this eventually for themselves, causing much amusement.

From the moment I arrived I was thrown in at the deep end. How I survived those first few days I shall never know. My shorthand dictation involved 2-8-0s, fish nuts, fish bolts, bogies and (surely not) nipples. There were DKWs (pronounced Ducks), something called Mulberry Harbour, Pluto, Bailey Bridges, pontoons, underwater reports, none of which I had ever heard of before. And it all required speedy transcription. At the same time I was given a book of about 300 abbreviations to memorise.

The carbon paper for duplicate sheets of typing was called 'ormig'. This became the bane of my life. Coloured a brilliant mauve, my warm hands frequently picked it up, to the delight of the men when I had an itch to scratch on my face. The result can be imagined, I must have looked like some native warrior, and it was not easy to remove.

When Sir Bernard Paget was replaced by Montgomery, GHQ became HQ21 Army Group and the flashes worn on our sleeves were replaced by the crossed swords. Practically all my typescripts were now headed 'Top Secret – Operation Overlord'; we returned to Hammersmith and, unfortunately, the London bombing. As the workload increased I was joined by two more ATS girls, Joyce and Jean.

Our office was a requisitioned house in Edith Road, bare of everything but the essential trestle tables and chairs, and it was very cold. Frozen fingers were not ideal for typing and we insisted we had a fire in the small grate in our room. A young army newcomer was given this duty; he managed to find some paper, wood and a few bits of coal, which we could hardly complain about given the fact these were all in short supply. Half an hour later our door was flung open by a sooty-faced CSM. His room was directly above ours and the chimney probably had not been swept for years.

It was not long before we were bombed out of there and we had to move further down the road. One of our very likeable officers and his wife, who was on a visit, died in this raid. One never knew from day to day what our own personal news would be; I was well aware of my family's vulnerability in these air raids as they too were in London.

We were no luckier in this second house for we were bombed out again, and the NCO on night duty was badly injured. We formed a chain the following morning, rescuing as much as we could. Halfway through, our Canadian officer appeared holding aloft a photograph of my sister's wedding (taken in June of that year) and which I kept on my desk. Everyone cheered. Working in these conditions it was amazing that HQ could carry on. The hard core were in St Paul's school.

We now moved to Nevern Mansions opposite Earls Court. The accommodation here was much more spacious, which was as well as more men and officers were being drafted in. Tn was now split into two. Another officer took over ports, docks and harbours, but I continued working for the D. Tn covering railways.

Every morning an Air Force NCO came in spreading on the table a map of the previous night's TAF (Tactical Air Force) targets. It was impossible not to be aware how important these targets were and how badly they had been damaged. Railway lines, stations, goods yards, and railway engines, damaged now but to be repaired later.

The longer carriage on my typewriter had to accommodate brief size sheets, as often lengthy columns of figures covered four of them and had to be lined up top to bottom and sideways. I really enjoyed tackling this challenge, and the satisfaction it gave me could never be achieved on a modern computer.

It was while we were at Nevern Mansions that we females had the option to volunteer for overseas service with HQ 21 Army Group, or be posted out. I would not like it to be thought I made any heroic decision to go dashing across the Channel and face the enemy head on, but after careful thought I volunteered. Interviewed by one of our ATS officers, I was told I was the youngest girl to volunteer.

It was shortly after this that Monty gathered us together in the Hammersmith Theatre, mentioned earlier, and reluctantly informed us it had been virtually impossible to recruit a sufficient number of male shorthand typists. It must have been one of the most difficult decisions for him to have made as he was very strong on principles. War, to him, was an all-male thing. But was it? Of course we would not be fighting, although not too far behind the front line. It was gratifying to realise we were important. The emancipation of women was not yet entirely in full swing.

Following this small gathering, another was called for the whole of 21 Army Group, for which the large Hammersmith cinema was taken over. This was presided over by the Chief of Staff, Major General Sir Francis W. de Guinqand. The importance of this meeting could mean only one thing – D-Day was imminent.

On the morning of 5 June 1944 we had the rare treat of being served eggs and bacon for breakfast, both of which were severely rationed throughout the UK. Our mess was situated in the basement of the Olympia, seating around 2,000, over which Taffy presided. He had obviously been given the go-ahead for a celebratory breakfast, which he had put into full swing before hearing later the landings had been delayed due to bad weather conditions in the Channel. The next twenty-four hours must have been horrendous for troops already in their landing craft in a heaving sea.

DO'S AND DONT'S

FOR

TROOPS GOING OVERSEAS

DO remember the enemy must have information and will stop at nothing to get it.

DO grasp that intelligence is built up by piecing together small items of information, like a jig-saw puzzle. You may consider that the scrap of information which you can give away is of no importance but it may supply the missing piece and reveal the whole plan.

DO understand that a breach of security instructions may cost your life, the lives of thousands of your comrades, and the success of a

MAJOR MILITARY OPERATION

That is why breaches of security, however trivial they may seem, are treated as

MOST SERIOUS DISCIPLINARY OFFENCES

SO,

DO pay attention when your officers explain Security Instructions. If you have seen the film " Next of Kin " you will understand the vital need for secrecy.

SOME DONT'S.

DON'T talk about your impending move.

DON'T give away :—your port of embarkation,
  the name of your ship or other ships in the convoy,
  the date or time of sailing,
  your destination or route, even if it's only a guess.

2

DON'T pass secret information to ANYONE—not even your family and lifelong friends. How can you expect them to keep it dark, when YOU have let it out to them ?

DON'T pose as one who knows.

DON'T be provoked by anyone's stupidity to show that you know better. He may not be as stupid as he looks.

DON'T hesitate to interrupt indiscreet talk or to report serious cases to your officers.

DON'T mind risking your popularity if circumstances demand it.

DON'T drink if you can't hold drink and your tongue too.

DON'T try to avoid censorship. Co-operate with it instead. It is designed to help you to take the enemy by surprise.

DON'T throw letters out of trains, and don't send telegrams or telephone messages on your way to, or at the port.

DON'T gossip with porters, travellers, stevedores or dock labourers before embarking, or with workmen on the ship.

DON'T try to smuggle letters or telegrams ashore from the ship. Use the post-boxes which are provided on board.

DON'T try to send messages in code. The enemy are better at reading codes than your pal or the girl you left behind you.

DON'T on arrival at your destination, hand letters to stewards or sailors on the ship to post when they get home. They are obliged to give them up before landing. You will merely be paying to get yourself into trouble.

FINALLY,

DON'T think that, because you hear someone else giving away secrets, it won't matter if you do the same. Two blacks don't make a white, and

DON'T assume the enemy knows it all already. He doesn't.

(2956.) Wt. 37453-8686. 500M. 11/43. A., P. & S., Ltd. 428.

6th June 1944.

SUPREME HEADQUARTERS
ALLIED EXPEDITIONARY FORCE

Soldiers, Sailors and Airmen of the Allied Expeditionary Force!

You are about to embark upon the Great Crusade, toward
which we have striven these many months.   The eyes of
the world are upon you. The hopes and prayers of liberty-
loving people everywhere march with you. In company with
our brave Allies and brothers-in-arms on other Fronts,
you will bring about the destruction of the German war
machine, the elimination of Nazi tyranny over the oppressed
peoples of Europe, and security for ourselves in a free
world.

Your task will not be an easy one. Your enemy is well
trained, well equipped and battle-hardened. He will
fight savagely.

But this is the year 1944 ! Much has happened since the
Nazi triumphs of 1940-41. The United Nations have inflicted upon the Germans great defeats, in open battle,
man-to-man.   Our air offensive has seriously reduced
their strength in the air and their capacity to wage
war on the ground. Our Home Fronts have given us an
overwhelming superiority in weapons and munitions of
war, and placed at our disposal great reserves of trained
fighting men. The tide has turned ! The free men of the
world are marching together to Victory !

I have full confidence in your courage, devotion to duty
and skill in battle. We will accept nothing less than
full Victory !

Good Luck ! And let us all beseech the blessing of Al-
mighty God upon this great and noble undertaking.

Dwight Eisenhower

Daily Mail

4 A.M. EDITION

BEAR BRAND STOCKINGS

NO. 15,006 ONE PENNY   FOR KING AND EMPIRE   WEDNESDAY, JUNE 7, 1944

BEACHHEAD WIDER AND DEEPER

Savage Fighting in Caen Streets: Front Now 100 Miles Across and Troops Still Pour In

THE first historic day of Europe's liberation has gone completely in favour of the Allies. "We have got the first wave of men through the defended beach zone and set for the land battle," said Admiral Ramsay, Naval C.-in-C., last night. "Naval ships landed their cargoes 100 per cent." Our troops and tanks are firmly ashore at many points along 100 miles of the Normandy coast from Cherbourg to Le Havre. They are ten miles inland at Caen; five miles inland at the base of the Cherbourg peninsula. The sea is rough on the beaches but reinforcements are pouring in.

German coastal batteries have been mostly silenced. Casualties among both airborne and assault landing troops have been much lower than expected. Losses at sea were "very, very small". Against the 7,500 sorties flown by the Allied Air Forces the Luftwaffe put in only 50.

1,000 'TROOP CARRIERS' IN FIRST AIR BLOW

TWENTY-FOUR hours have sufficed to smash the first fortifications of Hitler's vaunted West Wall. The Allied Navies and Air Forces, operating in unheard-of strength, have put the first wave of General Montgomery's armies safely ashore on the magnificent beaches of Normandy according to plan.

'Impregnable' strongpoints built up over three years by the famous Todt Organisation crumbled in a few hours under 10,000 tons of bombs and shells from 600 warships.

Minesweepers have swept away the mines. Engineers have cleared the underwater "fences", "pyramids", and "hedgehogs". Troops and guns and tanks are flowing on to the shores of France.

At Supreme Headquarters this morning there was a feeling of optimism that all was going well. Airborne operations, in which well over 1,000 planes and gliders took part, were particularly successful.

Weather was the biggest worry of the invasion commanders. A strong north-west wind sent white horses racing over a grey sea.

A naval officer back from the "front" said it made the heavy landing craft yaw from side to side, and its effect on the shallow beaches on either side of the Seine estuary was to raise a surge which drenched many of the troops from head to foot before they could reach the shore.

This added to the discomfort already produced by widespread seasickness. Up to yesterday afternoon the weather had shown no signs of moderating, but reinforcements and supplies continued to stream across the Channel.

PORTS AT RISK

Vessels carrying them, by canal, formed continuous lines right across the 100 miles of water from Normandy to the English coast.

German operation will stiffen now and on succeeding days but the first critical phase has been carried through by the matchless skill of our sailors, soldiers and airmen.

It is too early yet for the design of the invasion to take shape, but obvious objectives are the great ports of Cherbourg and Le Havre which in peace handled Transatlantic traffic.

Roughly half way between them, General Montgomery has struck for the town of Caen, 10 miles inland, which dominates roads and railways radiating all over Northern Normandy.

Mr Churchill said there was fighting in its streets.

Pilots returning late last night said our troops were moving inland. There was no longer any opposition on the beaches.

"We saw our tanks moving up on Caen. We could see no enemy infantry at this point near the coast."

The Germans report that Caen is the main invasion point. A big beachhead, they said, has been

morning. It shows our troops surging forward on a French beach.

Berlin Says Caen Air Coup Fails

'Exceptionally Grim Fighting'

BERLIN comment on the fighting up to early today was generally cautious, although Sertorius, the military commentator, claimed that an airborne coup against Caen had failed.

Early today the official News Agency gave this account of the fighting:

"Heavy fighting is in full swing. Some Anglo-American can paratroops who landed between Carentin and Bayeux, as well as airborne troops and seaborne troops, have been driven off in very heavy fighting.

"In the area of the Orne mouth the Anglo-American troops have been temporarily sealed off.

"Under the cover of heavy naval artillery the enemy is bringing up fresh troops.

"New actions by the Anglo-Americans can doubtless be expected but are not yet in evidence.

Defending stubbornly

"Fighting is exceptionally grim. The Anglo-American troops are defending themselves very stubbornly and are going all out to defend their positions."

The lack of German air support for the defenders was blamed on the weather.

Walter Farr, Daily Mail Special Correspondent, cabled from Stockholm last night: "I have been told the Berliners' faces show the demoralisation of bewilderment.

"'Sie Kommen, sie kommen!' ('They are coming') said the Germans to each other, gathered amid the ruins."

R.A.F. out again

Another great R.A.F. bomber force began to roar out from East Coast aerodromes as darkness fell last night, heading south.

MAP shows lay-out of D-Day operations, the beach-heads already established and where the paratroops landed. Little definite news has emerged so far. The Germans say we have established a beachhead 16 miles long on both sides of the River Orne, which leads to Caen.

Germans Execute 500 French Patriots

Daily Mail Special Correspondent

MADRID, Tuesday.

FIVE hundred French partisans and 'suspects' have been executed by Darnand's militia and the Gestapo for revolting against the Germans, according to reliable reports.

More mass executions are expected in the next few days.

This followed the German proclamation of a state of emergency in Paris. Many arrests have been carried out.

Many parks, including the Luxembourg Gardens, have been turned into camps where thousands are held under armed guard.

Barbed wire and machine-guns rut these parks off from the rest of Paris.

Drastic "martial law" orders have been broadcast by radio to all France.

Co-operation with the Allies is punishable by death and troops have been told to shoot at all persons ignoring a challenge.

First reports say the invasion caused wild excitement and in some areas the Germans have forbidden the population to leave their homes on any pretext.

START WAS 24 HOURS LATE

INVASION operations were postponed 24 hours because meteorological experts predicted that the weather would get worse.

They were right, but after a few hours they said an improvement was on the way.

The Allied commanders decided to act on this forecast and to proceed with the operations.

Again the "Met" men were right. If they had been wrong the operations might have been disastrous.

Swiss Get a Bomber

Two German bombers flew over Swiss territory yesterday; one was shot down.

5.27, AND NAVY WENT IN

First Cable from Invasion Fleet

From DESMOND TIGHE. Combined Press Reporter.

ABOARD A BRITISH DESTROYER OFF BERNIERES-SUR-MER Tuesday, dawn

GUNS are belching flame from more than 600 Allied warships. Thousands of bombers are roaring overhead, fighters are weaving through the clouds as the invasion of Western Europe begins.

Rolling clouds of dense smoke cover the beaches south-east of Le Havre as the full fury of the Allied force is unleashed on the German defences.

It is the most incredible sight I have ever seen.

We are standing 8,000 yards from the beaches of Bernieres-sur-Mer and from the bridge of this destroyer I can see vast numbers of naval craft of all types. They moved in to attack at 5.27 a.m.

Two forces are taking part – a British and Canadian unit under Rear-Admiral Sir Philip Vian, of Cossack fame, and an American task force under Rear-Admiral Alan G. Kirk. The air is filled with the continuous thunder of broadsides and the crash of bombs. Spurts of flame come up from the beaches in long snake-like ripples as shells range in to find their mark. It is exactly 7.25a.m., and through my glasses I can see

BACK PAGE — Col FOUR

LANDINGS SUCCEED

COMMUNIQUE No 2, from Supreme Headquarters issued at midnight, said the initial landings were successful. Here is the text:

Shortly before midnight on June 5 Allied night bombers opened the assault. Their attacks in very great strength continued until dawn.

Between 6.30 and 7.30a.m. two naval task forces commanded by Rear-Admiral Sir Philip Vian flying his flag in H.M.S. Scylla (Capt. T.M. Browning) and Rear-Admiral Alan G. Kirk in U.S.S. Augusta (Capt. E.H. Jones) launched their assault forces at enemy beaches.

The naval forces which had previously assembled under the overall command of Admiral Sir Bertram Ramsay made their departure in fresh weather and were joined during the night by bombarding forces which had previously left northern waters.

★

CHANNELS had to be swept through the large enemy minefields. This operation was completed shortly before dawn and while minesweeping flotillas continued to sweep towards the enemy coast, the entire naval force followed down swept channels behind them towards their objectives.

Shortly before the assault three enemy torpedo-boats made their departure in company attempted to interfere with the operation and were promptly driven off. The assault forces moved towards the beaches under cover of heavy bombardment from destroyers and other support craft. Reports show that our forces succeeded in their initial landings. Fighting continues.

Portugal Stops Wolfram

D-Day Decision

WASHINGTON, Tuesday.

PORTUGAL agreed, on the eve of the invasion, to stop all shipments of wolfram (tungsten) to Germany and to close down the wolfram mines, it was announced in Washington to-night.

Edward Stettinius, the U.S. Under-Secretary of State, disclosed that the United States, Britain, and Brazil co-operated in persuading Portugal to stop the wolfram trade.

The announcement said that the Portuguese Government undertook on June 5 to impose a total prohibition of exports of wolfram and also to cease production immediately.

BRITAIN RAID FREE UP TO 4 A.M.

Up to 4 o'clock this morning there were no reports of enemy activity anywhere over Britain.

MacA's MEN DRIVE ON IN BIAK

General MacArthur's communiqué said U.S. forces on Biak Island have now fought to within one-and-a-half miles of Mokmer airfield — A.P.

EXTRACT FROM 'THE STAR' dated
12 July 44

"Molly Gourlay's Mob" for Normandy

Miss Molly Gourlay, the golfer, now a Chief Commander in the ATS is, I hear, to be given command of all the ATS, Canadian WACs, and American WACs who are sent to France to serve under General Montgomery at Rear HQ of the 21st Army Group.

She will be the first woman officer to hold such an appointment in the field.

Miss Gourlay will, I imagine, have as her deputy a Canadian or American senior officer, for th plan set up for the men's services is being followed by the women. At SHAEF, for instance, British, American and Canadian women are all under the command of an American – Maj E.M. Davis, WAC, whose second in command is Senior Commander the Countess of Brecknock. These officers, as it chances, are of equal rank, but Major Davis is the senior.

More to Follow

Miss Gourlay, who speaks French, and will have many memories of golf at Le Touquet, was a VAD in the last war, joined the FANY in 1927 and in this way has been a quartermaster-sergeant and a quartermaster. Her special interest is motor transport – she has had a driving licence for more than 25 years.

She will have under her command in France, at first, a comparatively small contingent of officers and ATS but the number will later be considerably increased. The girls will do all manner of jobs, from driving staff cars and keeping a 24-hours-a-day drivers' pool going, to clerical, cooking, mess steward and orderly duties.

Their Own Red-Caps

First contingent will include four of their own despatch riders and a provost officer and a number of women Red-Caps. The duties of these Red-Caps are not yet clearly defined, but I know they are to give help to the French civilian population if asked to do so.

The girls will be fully mobile, even to having office accommodation on wheels, which they can move in a few moments.

The Continental Group

Official title of the girls will be the Continental Group, but they are already known as "Molly Gourlay's Mob" in the place where they are eagerly awaiting shipment overseas.

They have special "going abroad" kit, which includes a gas mask, water bottle and mess tin, and I am told they wear all of it with great pride.

Miss Gourlay's golf, of course, was virtually a procession of champion-ships, and she was champion of France three times. I well remember her beating Elsie Corlett, of Lytham and St Annes, six and four in the 36 holes final for the English Women's Championship at Woodhall Spa in 1926. Even in that foul weather Miss Gourlay was as unruffled as her beret.

"Could I have a new hat, please? After all, I've worn this for over a week!"

HISTORIC D-DAY TRIBUTE
Day by day this week we are reprinting the complete editions of the Mail from that momentous week 60 years ago. Here is your Day Two edition ...

Daily Mail

VI

4 A.M. EDITION

BEAR BRAND STOCKINGS

NO. 15,007   ONE PENNY   **FOR KING AND EMPIRE**   THURSDAY, JUNE 8, 1944

BAYEUX IS CAPTURED — OFFICIAL

First Town to Go, Cherbourg-Paris Road Cut

THIS is how the first American assault troops went ashore on the Normandy coast on D-Day. Warships put up a barrage, and the exploding shells, high up on the beach, formed a screen which hid the wading infantrymen from the enemy gun posts. The men, brought close in to the foreshore in the landing craft, waded the last hundred yards or so to dry land — and the maze of enemy tank traps — with their firearms slung on their shoulders.

5th Race North from Rome

From EDWIN TETLOW   On Highway 1, Wednesday

TWO columns of the Fifth Army are today forging ahead on the heels of disorganised Germans along the Via Aurelia (Highway One) and the Via Claudia, north-west of Rome.

One column is approaching Bracciano, 18 miles north, and the other is moving towards Civita Vecchia, 40 miles up the coast. The Germans are going so fast that our men are finding it difficult to keep contact.

A few rearguards, with machine guns, are the only enemy they meet and the pace of their advance is limited mostly by mine-fields and blown bridges.

In the last month the Germans have suffered such huge losses it is possible they may not have enough strength left to defend the Rimini-Pisa line.

Cooks and men of the supply battalions who were hurriedly given guns when Rome fell and told they were themselves part of fighting troops are among prisoners being taken.

HALIFAX IS MADE AN EARL

Birthday Honours

VISCOUNT HALIFAX, Britain's Ambassador at Washington since 1941 is created an earl in the Birthday Honours List, issued today.

Sir Henry J Wood, who celebrates his 75th birthday and 60th year of Promenade Concerts this week, becomes a Companion of Honour.

C Aubrey Smith, 81-year-old Hollywood actor, is made a knight.

EISENHOWER THERE, HOLDS BEACHHEAD TALKS

CAPTURE of Bayeux and the crossing at several points of the Bayeux-Caen road by Allied troops was announced by Supreme Headquarters at 1.30 this morning. The first step has been taken towards the isolation of the Cherbourg peninsula.

Bayeux, an old Norman town with a normal population of about 6,000, lies five miles inland. It stands athwart National Highway 13, from Cherbourg to Paris, and the main line railway.

Earlier the Germans reported that British were driving towards Bayeux from their beachhead in the Caen area after landing 100 tanks at one point.

In the second beachhead area on the Cherbourg peninsula American airborne forces were reported by the Germans to have linked up with troops landed from the sea.

General Eisenhower yesterday crossed the Channel to the beachhead area in a British warship, accompanied by Admiral Ramsay. For 4½ hours he cruised off the invasion beaches and held conferences with General Montgomery, Rear-Admiral Kirk, and field commanders, whose names are still secret.

After his return it was learned at Supreme Headquarters that the programme is working out as planned, and on time. The stern test of attack which may develop at any moment will be met with a full measure of confidence and material resources.

Last night the weather showed considerable improvement. The sea was said to be "fairly calm".

Tempo Rising, Savage Fighting Lies Ahead

From ALEXANDER CLIFFORD
21st Army Group H.Q., Wednesday

THE reports coming back to this headquarters from the Normandy beaches today build up to a rather more sober picture than yesterday. The triumph of having got ashore so swiftly and cheaply is behind us.

Now our invasion armies are facing up to the very real difficulties ahead.

But there is no reason to be dissatisfied with our progress so far. In the briefest possible language, this is the position.

We are ashore on all our beaches. All the beaches have been cleared; that is to say, they are no longer under direct small-arms fire.

They can, of course, still be shelled by medium and long-range guns.

Some of our beachheads have been linked up with the beachheads on their flanks. The tempo of the fighting is rising. We shall not continue to get away with such slight losses as we had yesterday.

It is obvious that yesterday we did not meet anything like an all-out effort by the Wehrmacht. Most of our

BACK PAGE — Col ONE

GERMAN HQ BLITZED

With S.H.A.E.F., Wednesday

A GERMAN Army headquarters less than 50 miles behind the battle line was demolished by US fighter-bombers this afternoon.

It was sighted carefully hidden in woods. Lightnings of the 9th Air Force made the attack with 1,000lb bombs from low altitude.

Bombs on E. Anglia

Enemy planes which crossed the East Coast in the night penetrated inland and some bombs were dropped. It is believed one raider was shot down.

BACK PAGE — Col ONE

BAYEUX IS LINK WITH 1066

BAYEUX, the first town on French soil to be liberated by the Allies, is famous for its link with the Norman invasion of 1066 — the Bayeux Tapestry, a strip of embroidery depicting the conquest of England by William of Normandy.

A quiet old-world town, it has a magnificent 13th-century cathedral with twin towers.

The town was sacked by Henry I in 1106 and was several times besieged during the Hundred Years' War and the religious wars of the 16th century.

Four-hours' Talks off Beachhead

Eisenhower Meets 'Secret' Chiefs

By STANLEY BURCH
ON A BRITISH WARSHIP
OFF THE BEACHHEAD
— Wednesday

FOR four and a half hours this afternoon General Dwight Eisenhower, with Admiral Sir Bertram Ramsay, Allied Naval Commander, cruised to and fro off the invasion beaches and held a series of conferences with operational commanders.

General Montgomery, Admiral Kirk, U.S. Naval Commander, and the commanders of the task forces have climbed aboard this warship and gone into immediate conference with General Eisenhower in the captain's cabin.

In this tremendous setting — surrounded by the anchored armada of thousands of ships — the Supreme Commander has secured the most up-to-date information of the battle-front situation within 30 hours of the first landing.

He undertook this audacious unescorted trip because he knew he could get more from personal meetings.

Shot RAF Men: Report Due

Mr Eden, Foreign Secretary, told MPs that a full report on the shooting of RAF officers in Stalag Luft III was being prepared by the German Government.

French Frontier Sealed

The Germans closed all French frontier posts in the Pyrenees at 10 last night. No one was permitted to enter or leave France.
—AP

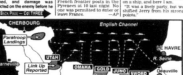

[Map labels: Allied Beachhead, Villers, CAEN, New Paratroop Landings Reported, Clecy, Flers, Argentan; CHERBOURG, Barneville, Paratroop Landings, St. Lo, UTAH, Link Up Reported, R. Vire, OMAHA, GOLD, JUNO, SWORD, BAYEUX, CAEN, LISIEUX, Paratroop Landings, LE HAVRE, R. Seine, Deauville, English Channel, 0 10 20 MILES]

BATTLE IS GROWING FIERCER

Communiqué No 4, issued from Supreme Headquarters AEF at 11.30 last night, stated:

ALLIED troops have cleared all beaches of the enemy and have in some cases established links with flanking beachheads.

Inland, fighting generally is heavy. An armoured counterattack in the Caen area on Tuesday evening was repulsed.

★

ENEMY resistance is stiffening as his reserves come into action.

The landing of troops and seaborne military supplies continues on all beaches, despite the north-westerly wind which has persisted since the assault.

Shortly before dawn today light coastal forces, while sweeping to the eastward, encountered a superior force of enemy craft.

Action was immediately joined, and damage was inflicted on the enemy before he

BACK PAGE — Col THREE

Sergeant is Back From a 'Party'

The first story of the fighting on the French beaches told by a British soldier comes from Sergeant George Maynard a Yorkshireman in a famous North Country division.

SERGEANT MAYNARD is one of the first British wounded to come back and this is his account of the encounter with the German defenders, which he describes as a "party".

"We landed soon after 7am. As our line of assault craft approached the shore, the Navy's guns were smashing shells into fortifications guarding the strip of the beach we had to take.

"Just ahead of us tank-landing crafts were already inshore and tanks raced up the shingle. German 88mm guns got on to them and there were several direct hits.

Swarming

"Jerry was fighting hard to stop us landing. Out across the beach was swarming with our chaps.

"We fought our way up a slope and got into wooded ground above. The wood was criss-crossed with low, stone walls, just like Sicily. There were Jerry snipers behind these walls and they let us have it.

"The chap next to me went down, shot through the neck. He was dead.

"We drove them out with Tommy guns and rifle fire and we advanced but they were causing us a lot of trouble.

'Very Hot Places'

"Then a grenade exploded at my feet. I got this smack in the head and was out of the battle. Jerries were by this time popping off with mortars.

"The beach and wood became very hot places. When Jerry went back a bit, still fighting hard, I made my way back to the beach and, with other wounded, was loaded on a ship, and here I am.

"It was a lively party, but we shifted Jerry from his strong points."
—AP

CHURCHILL TO GIVE NEWS

Statement Today

The Prime Minister will make a further statement on the progress of the Allied invasion, today (writes the Political Correspondent).

But this does not mean he intends to give daily reports. Only when there are important developments will he in future make statements.

HITLER VISITED BEACHHEAD

Hitler visited the beachhead in France two days ago, according to German prisoners quoted in a Press despatch from the "Western Front".

ROUEN IS POW CENTRE

Paris radio states that the first centre for British and American prisoners of war taken at the beaches has been set up at Rouen.

Her teeth are YOUR concern—

Every mother wants her children to grow up with strong, firm white teeth, *safe from the danger of decay*. The way to make sure of this is by giving the right care where they are young. Dentists advise the use of the one toothpaste containing 'Milk of Magnesia'*, which corrects acid mouth, so often the cause of dental trouble.

The toothpaste to ask for is Phillips' Dental Magnesia. Train your children to use it night and morning. They love its pleasant, mild flavour. Sold everywhere 1/1d. and 1/10½d.

Phillips' Dental Magnesia

TAKE OLD TUNES BACK TO THE SHOP

SUBJECT.   Collection of Kit ATS

6 Jul 44

All Auxiliaries TN.

The following orders must be complied with regarding kit:-

1.   2 Kit Holdalls only will be collected from Billets.

2.   They will be plainly marked with your name AND branch

3.   Kit will be stacked as under:-

MAIN PARTY 'A'

Kit will be stacked by 0800 hrs SATURDAY 8 JULY 44 in the following places:-

Personnel located in ARGYLL MANSIONS AND PALACE MANSIONS

In the hall of the back entrance in the Coy Office Block.

Personnel located in OAKWOOD COURT

In the hall of the entrance to Flats 3 and 4.

4.   PARTY 'B'

Kit will be stacked by 0800 hrs SUNDAY 9 JULY 44 same locations as in para 3.

5.   The following will stand by kits until they are loaded:-

Party 'A'	Oakwood Court	- Cpl Walker.
	Argyll Mansions	- Pte McNab.
Party 'B'	Oakwood Court	- L/Cpl Saville
	Argyll Mansions	- L/Cpl Dearmer

- 2 -

6.   The following infm is given. All bedding is being moved under Coy Office arrangements EXCEPT sheets, pillow cases and personal blanket whic will be packed with personal kit.

7.   It is hoped that all auxiliaries will help and co-operate as much as possible throughout the move.

                                                                SCMS.

Rear HQ 21 Army Gp
EWc

We on land were more fortunate, enjoying a second serving of bacon and eggs when the news was received on the morning of 6 June that this really was D-Day.

Those nail-biting early landings have been well documented; to those of us who lived and suffered the suspense, we had to face the reality of failure. Every possible eventuality had been meticulously thought out; it was now up to the troops. In Tn everything had been done not to overlook the smallest nut and bolt, replacement railway engines, everything required to erect the Mulberry Harbour, Bailey Bridges, etc. Right up to the last moment I was typing pages of revised figures. Railway engines would be shipped across the Channel (excellently reported and photographed in an edition of the *Railway Magazine* dated September 1999). The engine named *Longmore* shipped over to Calais later in 1945 was no doubt named after Longmore in Hampshire, where many of the Royal Engineers in Tn came from.

While we were still in Hammersmith it was considered a spot of PE would do us no harm. The thought horrified most of us; one could get pretty tired working quite long hours at times, followed by bombing raids at night. The PE instructor posted in for such an exercise was small, jolly and round, and a very nice person. I think we would have followed her anywhere except round the streets of Hammersmith, at least not in little brown shorts and top – and in the middle of winter.

The first day we made an effort. To be one of such a group running round the houses we felt such ninnies. Catcalls and whistles followed us everywhere until we reached the Olympia, where, to our horror, our PTI proceeded to take us up the fire-escape to the roof. Once there, in a howling wind and the risk of air raids, we did our 'jerks'. Never would we be so humiliated again. The next session, a few days later, commenced in the same way, but within the first five minutes our good-hearted instructor was blissfully unaware that her faithful band was thinning out. One by one we let her turn the corners while we ran straight on back to our billets. As these were opposite the Olympia we were able to watch the proceedings and wait for the return, when we joined up again for the last few yards. From then on everyone was satisfied: the powers-that-be, in the knowledge that our fitness was being ensured, our PTI who seemed blissfully unaware of her diminishing class, and we who worked from 8.30 a.m. to any late hour in the evening while work poured in six and a half days a week, were delighted to have an afternoon of enforced 'leave'. It was amazing at times how much the powers-that-be worried about us, to their complete satisfaction but with no apparent result as far as we were concerned.

By the end of June sufficient headway had been made in Normandy for preparations to leave the UK – or at least so we thought. But still Caen had not fallen to the liberation army. On 6 June 1944 we had each been issued with a letter from Eisenhower to his Soldiers, Sailors and Airmen or his Expeditionary Force. These 'morale boosters' were issued from time to time.

On 6 July we received written orders to 'Stand by our beds at 0800 hours on Sunday 9th July with our kit stacked. All bedding is being moved under Company Office arrangements EXCEPT sheets, pillow cases and personal blanket which will be packed with personal kits'; meaning we had to carry this ourselves. Our personal kit consisted of two officer-type kit bags, water bottle, steel helmet, respirator, great coat (more heavy than warm). These instructions were marked 'Top Secret' and all leave was cancelled. However, Rear HQ (as we were now called) were not heading for the French coast but Virginia Water and a longer wait than we had anticipated.

While still in Hammersmith we had been asked to confirm our next-of-kin and to make a will to be handed in. I explained I had been only sixteen when the war had started and now, at the age of twenty (before my birthday on 24 June) I had no chance to build up a fortune. But it was insisted upon. My thoughts were dwelling more seriously on the fact I might never have the chance to make another one later in life. I had my Slazenger tennis racquet, my sports model bicycle, a leather writing case from Fortnum & Mason and a few savings certificates.

Time was also enlivened (or should I say suffered) having our overseas inoculations. I found these particularly painful when my arm looked infected and became inflamed. The MO (Medical Officer) pronounced this to be a good sign as it showed the jab had taken very well. Sick Bay was usually to be avoided at all costs, but this time it was unavoidable and the MO and medical orderlies had a field day.

Also, while we had been in Hammersmith, our CO (who we understood had been a 'deb') arranged for us to have a greatly reduced price perm and cut at Vasco's in Dover Street, London. I had a Bubble Cut, which would last a long time. My hair was cut very close to my head and my forage cap (worn when off duty) sat on the top like a drunken ship in a rough sea. No one could speak to me for days.

Joyce and I were billeted in a lovely house called 'High Trees' in Sunningdale with a natural lake for swimming. Availing ourselves of this delight we would then go down to Lady Webb's canteen for a cup of cocoa. Our emergency rations, accompanying our water bottles, comprised some solid hard 'dog' biscuits and chocolate as hard as iron, which we might at some future date be glad of. Some Dutch courage, too, no doubt.

Meanwhile the battle for Caen continued around Villers Bocage. Rumour had it much of the delay was caused by disagreement between Eisenhower and Montgomery. It is said that 'two heads are better than one', which may not have been the case here. As far as the men we worked with were concerned, trust in Monty was supreme. Difficult? Maybe.

During July, when there continued to be a delay in progress on the frontline, there were more rumours that Montgomery felt the troops needed a boost to their morale, and moving his HQ to Normandy would be an indication of his optimism, regardless of the slow progress being made. In the event, we packed and were ready to leave Surrey in the early hours of a morning at the end of July.

Chapter 3

We left Virginia Water around 5 a.m. When the trucks arrived I was fortunate to be the last one to climb aboard. This was always a favoured seat, as inside it was impossible to see the view; I now had a good view of the beautiful sunrise and the lovely English countryside we were leaving.

As all leave had been cancelled over the past weeks while awaiting embarkation, I was now reliving the last short leave of twelve hours we had been allowed prior to this. We had been forbidden to mention (or show) any indication to our families that we were being posted abroad. In any case, even to us, postings abroad could mean anywhere. However, we were pretty sure our destination was Normandy; in fact we just *knew*, otherwise how could the Liberation Army possibly do without us! That visit had caused a lump in my throat.

Southampton was heaving with troops. In comparison we were such a small contingent of girls: shorthand typists, clerks, two hairdressers, etc. After sandwiches and tea we were photographed by the press and interviewed, then led out to board our ship, one of a long convoy crossing that afternoon. It was somewhat unnerving to see such an old vessel looking as though it had been mothballed since the First World War. It was already crammed with over 6,000 Canadians aboard, embarrassingly watching us struggling to negotiate the plank with all our kit. There was a great deal of amusement among them when one of us lost our kit overboard and a member of the crew had to dive in to retrieve it. No, it wasn't me!

We understood we would be landing that evening. With all our gear – two full kitbags, steel helmet, great coat, respirator, water bottle, weighing heavily, Joyce and I sat down on the deck with relief as the ship set sail. It was a pleasant summer afternoon, but there was a sense of unreality about it. None of us had ever been abroad and this was no tourist trip. We may have lived through the London bombing, but the other side of the Channel was a new dimension of this war.

Stretching our legs during the afternoon we could see a coastline in the distance. Our common sense should have told us we could not be there yet; nevertheless, we all began to gather up our gear, only to be informed by the crew that the rear part of the convoy had had to return to the Isle of Wight and what we could see were the Needles. The Channel had been mined again and had to be cleared before we could proceed.

As we had left Virginia Water in the early hours we were tired and hungry and the crew directed us down to the hold for something to eat. Not a large area, it was already overcrowded by girls ahead of us. It was extremely hot, smelt revolting, and we looked at the latrines in disbelief. These were obviously well known to seafarers but we had never seen anything like them, with no privacy whatsoever, lined up along a wall on a high platform. We were certainly hungry, but preferred to make our escape as soon as possible. In any case we heard provisions were far short of feeding even our small number, and they were not at all palatable.

By now it was getting dark. The earlier part of the convoy had made the crossing but we who had had to return to the Isle of Wight were motionless. Joyce and I decided we would put our heads down on our greatcoats and spend the night on deck, but we were rudely awakened by a voice insisting we move, unless, of course, we wanted to be drenched in the early morning hours by the crew carrying out their normal routine of hosing down the decks. But where could we go? The booming voice took us along to the Smoking Room, which we would have to vacate at dawn. Overcoming the intense smell in there, we thanked him profusely, and stretched out on the seating.

In the morning we again approached the hold, but not with the unpalatable food in mind. After a hilarious use of the toilet facilities, we decided to sit out on the deck and open one of our emergency rations and suck a piece of the rock hard bar of chocolate. Later, our very nice 'booming voice' brought us a cup of tea and a sandwich.

The ship was now moving forward slowly behind another which was only just visible in a thick fog. As the mist lifted, I began to feel seasick. Joyce disappeared to report this to our CO and returned with some pills, which, apparently, were much in demand. Unfortunately, these made me feel sleepy and half an hour later I was ready to doze off when we heard an emergency drill was being organised. I had the dickens of a job getting into my Mae West (life-saving jacket). Being teetotal I had never had a hangover, but Joyce said I gave a good imitation of having one.

Chapter 4

It was late that evening, after thirty-six hours on board, that we finally were able to prepare for landing on the Normandy beach at Arromanches, but as we were still some way out at sea the last lap was made in landing craft. I had typed much about the Mulberry Harbour and regretted that the opportunity now to view it was past my caring. We were all very tired as we headed for the lorries waiting to take us to Bayeux. It was a bit unnerving to hear gunfire in the distance, the sky intermittently lit up, as we travelled towards it.

The road, badly pitted, was bumpy. Eventually, we turned into a field, which we heard later was an apple orchard. We literally fell out of the lorry with all our kit and in the blackout, voices directed us towards some tents. We were totally unaware that the canvas was not covering level ground, but was over deep dugout squares containing three beds each. With girls ahead of us we heard squeals of surprise as they disappeared inside the deep drop. The beds were surprisingly soft, and Joyce and I littered our third bed with our kit and were soon fast asleep.

Never was a breakfast more welcome, and arrangements had been made for it to be available to us all the following day, no matter what time we woke up; in our case it was about noon. Bread was of poor quality back in the UK and I was to learn later it was no better in France, but that first morning on foreign soil the mess officer, Taffy, had set up a large marquee and produced the most delicious breakfast imaginable. The smell of fresh bread, eggs, bacon, tea (very hot) was wonderful. It was a meal fit for a king. How lucky we were, as in no way could any of the soldiers in the initial stages of the D-Day landings have enjoyed such a welcome feast. While remaining slight, weighing around 8 stone and just over 5 foot 3 inches tall, I always enjoyed my food.

Facilities for washing were catered for with a bowl of water behind a hedge and at this stage more than welcome. An improvement to this arrangement came a few days later when army sappers fixed up a large tent containing overhead pipes with holes at intervals. Each of us stripped and stood under one of these holes shouting 'Ready', while the sapper outside pumped away. Initially the water was cold, but improved later to hot and cold. Mischievously, the sapper would alternate it too much one way or the other to our shrieks of 'too hot' or 'too cold'. I do not think there was any shortage of sappers volunteering for this duty.

The men had travelled separately from us and had arrived a day or two earlier. Tents in a nearby field had been put up to house officers and ORs, and I had a small tent to myself. As a protection against inclement weather, we had been provided with metal covers for our typewriters, which proved to be utterly useless. To work smoothly, our machines needed a warm dry atmosphere, and this was far from the case under canvas during cold damp nights. My shorthand notebook fared little better when the paper became damp in these conditions. Our kit, which had been so meticulously thought out, omitted one important item – wellington boots. In the outbreaks of heavy rain our shoes were totally inadequate to wear in the resultant mud, and an urgent supply had to be sent for from the UK. These problems were endured alongside broken nights from the continuing distant gunfire and the possibility of flak raining down on our canvas tents, but everyone was very cheerful.

Before leaving the UK our additional kit had included a good supply of DDT powder, which we were instructed to use abundantly along all the seams in our clothing and skirt hems. From now on any type of skin rash would be attributed to tiny black things called fleas which apparently enjoyed conditions across the channel. 'Normandy Tummy' (our name for dysentery) was also playing havoc amongst us. On the hot dry days the wind blew fine sandy dust over the food in the mess tent creating this highly unpleasant result. Large white pills were handed out in enormous quantities.

Bayeux was pathetically war-torn. General de Gaulle had paid the town a visit on 20 June when I am sure all the local population would have been out to welcome him, but when we walked up the main street it had a deserted air. We had all been warned not to avail ourselves of the local cider, which I understand was very potent; nor were we to eat any of the apples grown in the orchard where we were billeted. With the recent fighting and hordes of troops passing through, one could well imagine the local inhabitants might have been glad of their cider and, no doubt, able to deal with the strength of it.

Having some time off one afternoon, Joyce and I took advantage of going further afield, a trip which was to be a sobering experience. On our way to Villers-Bocage early in August, we were taken along lanes lined with small white crosses, each one indicating a temporary burial during recent fighting. There were so many of them. That fierce attacks, for every inch of the way, had taken place was clearly evident everywhere. The D-Day landings and the liberation were never going to be a pushover; June and July 1944 were to prove this.

In strong contrast to the above, a 'cinema' was erected for us; a large canvas tent fitted out with wooden benches. The showing of old films was constantly interrupted by much shouting and clapping when the projector broke down, as it did frequently. Compare this with the high profile concerts put on for the American troops. Joyce and I had the opportunity to enjoy one of these; they certainly knew how to entertain, flying over Hollywood celebrities while hundreds of their troops sat on the grass in front of the huge stage enjoying a break from the frontline.

One afternoon Joyce and I were wandering around Bayeux when we passed a small old-fashioned French cinema. A Bing Crosby film was billed outside and we thought it would be fun to go in. A few French francs found us making our way upstairs. The film had started and, coming in from outside, we were unable to see in the dark. In order not to disturb anyone we felt for two unoccupied seats bordering the aisle and sat down to enjoy the film. Imagine our surprise, (and amusement), when the lights came on at the end of about an hour and a half to find we were in complete isolation, the only two people in the balcony.

Such incidents, and certainly the more unpleasant dysentery, broke up the air of waiting for something to happen, which would involve us work-wise. There was not a great deal keeping me busy. If there was concern among our Royal Engineer officers regarding the lack of progress around Caen, they showed no signs of it.

Eventually the long-awaited breakthrough was made. I was called in to see Major Stewart-Fergusson. Even by army standards I was not prepared to hear that a detachment of some of the men and officers was going forward the following morning to Rouen. Col. Fitch would be in control of all Railway Operating Groups and Companies reinstating the badly damaged railway system, in association with the SNCF, and would be requiring a shorthand typist. I had been asked for. This was going to be very exciting, but when I heard I would be the only female I had questions to ask about my billet and travelling arrangements. The former was not arranged until we actually arrived in Rouen, and the latter I had no complaints about – I would be travelling with the Colonel, his driver and two other officers in the Humber, not with the men in their lorry.

I was sorry to be parted from Joyce and Jean, but for the time being I said my goodbyes to both. I was not sorry to say farewell to the huge army of insects that had wormed their way through the canvas lining our 'dugouts'. They had not been a particularly welcome sight when I opened my eyes each morning.

Caen before the war.

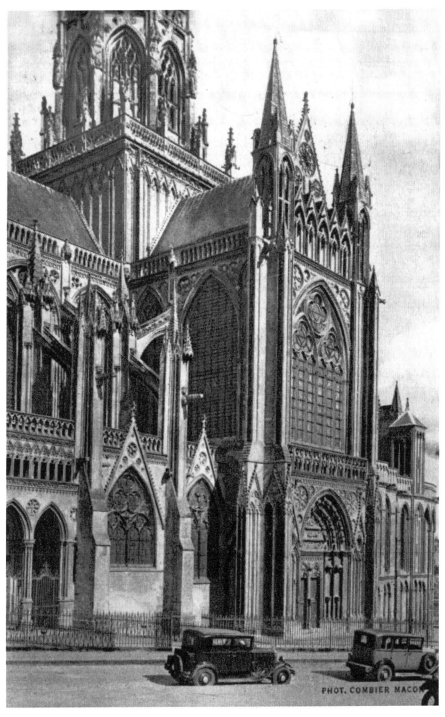

PHOT. COMBIER MACON

Bayeux Cathedral before the war. Bayeux was a very war-torn area when we arrived.

The interior of Bayeux Cathedral before the war.

Caen was an area of fierce fighting and we were well aware of this when we heard the shrapnel coming down around our apple orchard in Bayeux.

Eglise Saint-Pierre, Caen.

Chapter 5

We left the following morning at 9 a.m. The Normandy countryside would obviously take some time to recover from the activities of the past few weeks. Cows, always tethered, grazed on some of the farmland, but there was an absence of any of the usual farming expected during August.

I settled in the back seat of the Humber, making a note of our journey: Vaucelles, Tilly, Villers-Bocage (what was left of it), Caen, across the River Orne, Pontefract, Dozule-Potol, Pont l'Eveque, Pont Beuzeville, Pont Audemer, Sotteville. Here we stopped with our sandwiches and tea, and made use of the hedges on both sides of the road; this was not a toilet country, as I was to find out on many occasions. I am not sure this particular route would have been the straightest in normal circumstances, but allowance had to be made for diversions.

At around 1800 hours we reached the outskirts of Rouen. All three bridges across the Seine had been severely damaged, and the single narrow Bailey Bridge provided for one-way traffic only. The queue on both sides of the river was miles long. The Red Caps (military police), spotting the Colonel's pennant on the bonnet of his vehicle, stopped all traffic in both directions and waved us across from the back of the queue, much to the enjoyment of this particular occupant. If this was going to be the good life I very much looked forward to it. A dream soon shattered. As soon as we left the bridge, I noticed the whole area down by the river was heaving with military personnel, like a busy ants' nest.

While the men were taken to their billets and my officers left the car, the major alone was left to escort me to accommodation in 45 Rue de Buffon, where a French couple had agreed to billet me. My heart sank when we stopped outside what looked like a fortress, fronted by large iron gates. After clanging the bell (enough to awaken the dead), my officer escorted me across the large cobbled courtyard, knocked at a door in one corner, introduced me to Mme Médard, said I would be called for at 8.30 the next morning, and left.

I greeted Madame in French, which, unknowingly to her, was all that came to mind in the rush over the past twenty-four hours. Having the mistaken impression I was fluent in her language, I was unable to follow her part of the ensuing conversation. She was tall, austere, and somewhat forbidding to this twenty-one-year-old. Realising I was not getting the gist I discovered she could speak fluent English. Her husband, not available at the moment, was a local pastor. The only other member in the household was Madeleine, their home help, the same age as me.

This corner accommodation was one of the many tenements surrounding the courtyard. Despite it being the month of August, it was very cold, being built of stone. The solid stone staircase led up to my bedroom, not particularly clean and, like the rest of the house, sparsely furnished. The only toilet, like the wash basin, was somewhat primitive.

I was feeling rather hungry and after a wash in the basin and a tidy up I went downstairs. I could only assume that the obviously hurried arrangements that had been made would include a meal, at least on this first night. I found Madame in their living room in earnest conversation with someone who, although not in uniform, looked every inch an authoritative Englishman. I was offered a seat while they continued their earnest conversation in voluble French. I eventually excused myself and went into the kitchen, but there was no evidence of a meal being prepared. There was nothing for it, but to go to bed and look forward to breakfast.

Going down at 7.30 a.m., I found the table being cleared by Madeleine and no-one else about. Indicating to Madeleine I was hungry and thirsty (she spoke no English) she produced a saucer with some paté and a saucer of jam, part of a French loaf and the tiniest piece of butter, as well as a very strong black coffee with no sign of any milk. I did my best to look pleased and fulfilled.

Rouen. One of the destroyed bridges. How lovely this city must have looked before the war.

Rouen. All these bridges were destroyed. We entered across a Bailey Bridge catering for single-line traffic only in September 1944.

Le Pont Transbordeur, Rouen.

Les Quais, Rouen.

Eglise St-Over, Place de l'Hotel-de-Ville, Rouen.

Palais de Justice, Rouen.

Above: The view of Rouen from the hillside.

Left: The tower where Joan of Arc was imprisoned. I passed this every morning, but I believe it is no longer there.

Madeleine with her brother.

Madeleine Cottard, the maid in Mme
Médard's home, where I was billeted.

When I told my Royal Engineer escort, who had come to collect me, that
I was surprised this household were such early risers, and that I had been
ready and waiting for him for the past hour, he said he had no intention of
being any earlier as their breakfast was at 7.30 a.m. and our 'office' was on
the other side of town.

My return back that evening was even more puzzling. I decided I would
join the men in their mess in future and arrive back around 8 p.m. To our
amazement there was no sign of life, and the loud clanging of the bell for
someone to open the gate did indeed 'wake the dead'. My army escort left
me to face the many irritated tenants, opening their windows shouting in
no uncertain terms that my 'late' arrival was not exactly welcome. It was all
very odd.

All finally came to light when it was discovered that I was working to
the Army's British time but living with French time. This was not only a
one-hour difference, but a two-hour one, taking into account the different
summer times. There was nothing anyone could do about this as I was the

only one affected by it. My morning escort, however, was not agreeable to continue his duty and Madeleine asked whether she could walk with me across the centre of the town each morning. This was an ideal arrangement and my French improved considerably. Madeleine was obviously not the military escort I was supposed to have, but it was becoming apparent that such arrangements were being left to me.

French was a language poorly taught way back in the 1930s and not considered to be an important subject, earning the British the reputation for never being able to converse in anything but English. At my college we had had a somewhat weird French teacher who, in his view, was more forward thinking. If we sat and listened to a constant replaying of the latest pop records we would learn more conversational French. Well, it was a very enjoyable lesson listening to 'J'attendrai, Hallo, hallo James, Quelle Nouvelles?' etc. with Tino Rossi and Jean Sablon belting them out, but I was now finding this of little use to me; this was not the way to greet Mme. Médard or her husband.

Having always enjoyed history, both as a school subject and by reading, I was obviously looking forward to seeing the great historic town of Rouen. Unfortunately, I was not there as a tourist and with just one half day off in every seven I was unable to explore as I would have wished. In any case, as in Bayeux, France was very much a war-torn country, not as much bombed as London and Coventry, but there was a sense that they were slowly waking up to their regained freedom. The departure of the German army had been not much more than days before, following a long occupation.

The walk through the centre of Rouen took us past the tower where Jeanne d'Arc had been imprisoned and the location of the stake where she had been burned to death. Beneath the famous bridge, connecting both sides of the road, were interesting small shops. I was learning much about the Médard family from Madeleine. It appeared there had been an active pocket of resistance centred around the Rue de Buffon during the German occupation. My arrival followed shortly after the Germans had left and the family were very concerned that their eldest daughter had been arrested and taken with them. I began to realise the anxieties and fears they had suffered, not only recently but over the past five years.

Our office was a requisitioned house in Rue de Bouquet, where I sat busily typing the Colonel's orders to the Railway Operating Groups and Companies, surrounded by the rest of the detachment. They were a lively mixed bunch; our towering Scottish Sergeant, very small 'Dickie Bird', our CSM who had been employed as a clerk in a Law Court in Civvy Street, and who wanted me to teach him shorthand, which would improve his chance of promotion on his return, Frank, our Welsh miner from South Wales, and Jim who greatly missed his wife and young son who was growing up without him. I was never sure what they all did, but the officers were busy, involved as they were in the important reinstatement of the railways improving the L of C (line of communication) across northern France into Belgium and eventually Holland. Now and again I accompanied one or two of the officers to the main railway station and could see for myself just what an involved reinstatement this was. Back in Hammersmith I had worked among Royal Engineers who had trained at Longmore, many of whom were probably now busily employed here and elsewhere along the line.

On Saturday 7 October 1944, General de Gaulle came to Rouen and M. et Mme Médard were invited to attend a service in the Cathedral and a dinner for special guests afterwards, indicating they had had some particular involvement during the occupation, or their daughter had. I attended the service with them, but obviously not the dinner.

I had grown fond of Madame who began to thaw towards me. My impression was that she had grown to trust no one, not even me when I first arrived. I saw very little of Monsieur, which was understandable considering the difficulty I had regarding my juggling with their time and mine.

Two or three days later after General de Gaulle's visit, we were moving on from Rouen to Amiens. Having hugged and kissed the Médards goodbye and Madeleine, who had become a good friend, I never saw them again. Madeleine and her mother kept in touch with me for some years; she later left Rouen to go to Switzerland to help with the rehabilitation of the hundreds of orphaned children from all over Europe.

I left with one particular memory on that day. While working in Rue de Bouquet my desk was alongside a French window and recently a young French naval officer had been home on leave at his home opposite. While trying to concentrate on my work the men teased me mercilessly about him. He certainly appeared to show a great deal of interest whenever I was sitting at my typewriter.

While the men were packing everything up he came across while I waited for the Humber outside. With a charming smile, so typical of French males, he handed me a bag of tomatoes. This was so totally unexpected my face turned a colour to match and I was totally speechless. He was quite serious and asked whether he could write to me. Sidestepping this, I asked whether he would like to write something in my small autograph book, which he did and which I still have. A long time later I was told tomatoes were a typical love gift in France given by an admirer. I hope I wasn't having my leg pulled.

Chapter 6

Cooperation with the SNCF reinstating the railway through to Antwerp continued at a fair pace. Reports, orders and instructions were continuing to be issued as before. We arrived in Bvde Thiers late afternoon and my first view of the tall old building that was to be our office was not encouraging. I would be sharing a large room on the ground floor with the men, and the officers would be on the floor above. The only toilet in the backyard was disgustingly primitive. The men, as usual, were cheerful, bringing in the inevitable wooden trestles and chairs.

Across the road Major Stewart-Fergusson introduced me to my new billet and adopted family. It was a warm, comfortable house behind a small courtyard, and my welcome equally warm. M. Busseuil was a vivacious character and would prove to be a great tease. Madame was small and motherly; her mother, Grandmère Hélène, I was to learn, had not been pleased when their previous lodger, a German, had had to depart in a hurry shortly before I arrived. She had grown rather fond of him and now I was to have the bedroom he had occupied. Berthe was their Spanish maid who kept very much in the background, and was no longer a young woman.

My bedroom was warm and comfortable, something I would appreciate during the coming severe winter, already on the way early in October. There was a very nice bathroom, but again only a poor toilet adjoining the kitchen downstairs. I was to discover they were great entertainers of their many friends. I settled in immediately, as I could well imagine their German had before me. I suspected this household would have been happy to welcome anyone who happened to be 'passing through', and Madame Busseuil soon became my 'Maman Française'.

That first evening of my arrival was an event to celebrate. The major, captain and myself were joined by their neighbour, M. Legrand and a M. et Mme Plantard. The large table in their dining-cum-sitting room was laden with a feast of wonderful food. I was to discover later that Monsieur was in the farming business. There was no evidence of the austerity I had seen in my previous billet. Not one of this family could speak English. Grandmère Hélène struggled with one word – 'sugaarr' – having difficulty controlling her set of false teeth. My difficulty in pronouncing, correctly in French, 'Cathedral' was greeted with peels of laughter.

Outside their homes I don't think Amiens at that time was a particularly interesting place. Amiens, like Rouen, was another historic town, and at that stage of the war was no tourist attraction. There were no obvious signs of the destruction experienced in the large cities and towns in the UK. Any bombing across northern France had been aimed at specific targets with no indiscriminate attacks on the local population such as the German bombing of London, Coventry etc.

I missed the cheerful spirit that I had left behind in London, despite the heavy loss of life, rationing, nights of heavy bombing, the sound of an air-raid warden whistling a happy tune while German planes droned overhead. I think the existence in any invaded country had been intolerable and taken its toll on the population. We also had three wonderful morale boosters – Churchill, Montgomery and Eisenhower, although it must have been very difficult for them at times.

While my busy fingers tapped away and my notebook was always at the ready, as a detachment the men had little to do in the evenings. Discovering a spare room on a higher floor above the officers' work rooms, we found a large empty room with a dart board. Forming two teams we began competing against each other. These turned into some very enjoyable evenings, and we also found some old records that were great fun to listen to.

The mess was shared with a large contingent of Royal Engineering workforce whose vocabulary certainly widened the extent of my own. In such an all male atmosphere, I was aware that I was not particularly welcome when the men from our detachment asked them to watch their language in front of me. Assuring them I was not going to let this worry me I was virtually ignored.

A smaller mess for the detachment alone was run by a funny little cockney cook and his French equivalent. They chatted away in a language all their own, interspersed with 'Avez-vous any cornee beef', which never seemed to relate to anything while they carried on cooking. They went to a lot of trouble to make a 'dart board' cake for the winning teams. I am not sure what went into them, but we always demolished them without any grave effect.

Meanwhile, Madame allowed me in and out of the house during the day, either to pick up something I needed or use their somewhat better toilet. These unplanned visits could sometimes bring me closer to the French way of life. Working seven days a week with a half-day off (this included Sundays) I popped across one Sunday morning and was horrified to see a large hairy animal lying dead in the courtyard, still bleeding profusely. Monsieur, I was to learn, enjoyed wild boar hunting, his prey finally ending up on my breakfast plate as paté. In no way could I eat this 'delicacy' after that.

Another time I walked into the kitchen when the local doctor was treating Madame. I knew or had heard that the continentals were less inhibited about these things. When I turned to leave hurriedly I was introduced to the doctor and asked to stay while he gave my hostess an injection in her derrière.

The Busseuils were a lovely gregarious family and through them I met many of the local celebrities. Their neighbour, M. Legrand, was particularly interesting. He was an artist who had exhibited in Paris. One of his exhibits caught my eye and he asked whether I liked it. I have always enjoyed paintings depicting children, as this one did. A few days later he gave me a photograph of it, and although not in colour I can still look at it.

Two visitors to the house were schoolteachers who were anxious for me to see their home and school. They were talented and very upset that their grand piano had been damaged when their home had been searched by the Germans. At the school I was asked to answer questions from the children. I said I would but only on the condition that these were to be about my own school days prior to the war. This was due to the continued 'Talk Costs Lives' campaign. They were very well behaved and intelligent. My photograph was taken and later displayed in the hall. Another of the regular visitors to the house was a countess, but I never discovered the origin of her title; again, she was an interesting character.

Although invited frequently by the Busseuils to dinner in the evenings, I avoided this as often as I could as I had no idea how my hosts were being compensated. I, myself, had received no pay since leaving Bayeux. On one occasion I was invited to dinner with two of my officers, when the tricky subject of payment was discussed. I am not sure how this was resolved, but it gave me the opportunity to mention the lack of my own. The men attended Pay Parade each week, signed the mile-long sheet, saluted and smartly turned about. But there was no pay sheet for me.

No one had queried this on my behalf, until now. Not only did a mile-long pay sheet arrive for me, but it was brought from Brussels by an ATS officer who had been sent with some replacement items from stores, and a particularly urgent monthly requirement, which at that time was extremely bulky. I am not sure she entirely approved of the beret I wore instead of the ATS peaked cap, but her visit was brief and she made no further comment. It was an army issue beret the men wore. With some money now in my pocket I was keen to spend it. For some time, on my window-shopping excursions through the town, I had had my eye on a fine gold chain bracelet.

Although I never came across them myself, I understood there were pockets of resistance against the allies, whether by some remaining Germans or even French, and for this reason I had to notify an officer whenever I was going to wander abroad. This was no hardship as I enjoyed any of the men's company when they were detailed to accompany me. So, with two or three of them, we set off for the jewellers.

I pointed out the bracelet I wanted to purchase but this was refused. It was explained to me even such a very small amount of gold was not being allowed out of the country, unless of course I could provide the equivalent in exchange. I could almost sense the salesman was rubbing his hands in glee, even more so when I produced my Parker pen and asked whether the gold nib, if removed, would be acceptable. Oh yes, it certainly was. I knew I could have the nib replaced back home but I had a suspicion he had worked a better deal than I had.

While in Amiens I had made friends with two youngsters. Josianne Glachant (ten) stopped me one morning to ask whether her mother could do my laundry. The only charge was my army issue of a bar of soap. I was delighted, and my shirts were returned beautifully cleaned and ironed. I thought my soap was being put to good use until one evening I came across a number of local women slapping their washing on the large stones beside the canal, among them Josianne's mother, with my army shirts, and not a bar of soap to be seen. The result was very impressive. Although I never visited Josianne's home, she lived at 44 Rue Blind de Bourdon.

The other young friend, Ghislain Adam who was about sixteen, approached me to say her parents would be very pleased if I and one of the soldiers would join them for a meal one evening. The men in particular enjoyed these invitations. I myself was doing rather better; probably I was more of a curiosity in a town bursting at the seams with male khaki uniforms. In the event, I asked our Sergeant 'Jock' whether he would like to accept this invitation with me.

M. et Mme. Adam's house was on the outskirts, near a narrow gauge railway. They welcomed us warmly. Ghislain's mother had gone to a great deal of trouble to provide a delicious meal, finishing with oeufs à la neige. Unlike the UK there was no lack of eggs here in France, even though soap was in short supply.

M. Adam related to us his activities, living in Petain's free French area in the South of France during the occupation. We had to get the gist of it, following his excitable French, which ended with him holding his knife under his chin, giving a good imitation of slitting someone's throat, accompanied with a loud 'les Boches'. A good display of play-acting or had he actually carried this out? We were glad when this excitable little man put down his knife. Madame Adam followed this by dealing out some cards, getting us to hold hands and close our eyes, while the table mysteriously rose and fell. It was an entertaining evening.

Chapter 7

We were still in Amiens as Christmas approached. It was bitterly cold, with constant snowfalls. On most mornings I was glad office and billet were opposite each other. There were two situations I would have been pleased (or preferred) to be in over the Christmas – either to hear we were going on to Brussels or being given leave to spend it with our families at home. Neither materialised.

Christmas Day was not a festive occasion in France, whereas New Year's Eve was. On Christmas morning I was invited next door, together with the Busseuils, for a glass of wine. M. Legrand's company was always interesting, as was his home. The rest of the day the detachment worked as usual, with a darts match in the evening and the BBC radio programmes on.

New Year's Eve I accepted an invitation to join the Adams, mainly because this was going to be at a relative's home in another part of Amiens and it was an opportunity to meet some fresh faces. Permission to go was granted by the officers providing I kept to the military curfew, and returned at the latest by 11 p.m. This was not as unusual as it sounds for in the part of the UK I came from – the south-east – Christmas, not New Year, was celebrated. I never recall seeing in the New Year before the war.

It was a long walk across to this family's house. As we approached a great deal of noise could be heard, and we had difficulty getting in as we squeezed our way into a house bulging at the seams. There was much kissing and hugging, and I soon lost contact with my friends. Knowing no one else did not matter at all to anyone, and it was almost impossible to hold a conversation. I did catch sight of one other uniform from time to time, a young airman, but had no chance to speak to him. In any case, he did not appear particularly happy for some reason. Maybe, like me, he found it all rather overwhelming, but to them it was virtually their first Christmas of freedom and the end of their war, while in the UK I knew that my family were still suffering air raids from those deadly V1s and V2s.

Recovering my breath, I followed the push towards their large dining room where the table was laden with food. It was not long before someone started singing 'Les Marseillaise' and they all joined in with gusto. Seeing my uniform, and for my benefit, this was followed by 'God Save the King'. And so it continued first one and then the other. I would have preferred 'Auld Lang Syne' and an end to the evening. What was I saying? In horror I realised it was midnight.

My anxiety to leave now spread, until someone suggested my friends accompanied me back, but I knew our Redcaps would be on the look out for any khaki uniforms. A coat was found for me and everyone left with us, a singing rowdy mob making our way across town with me hidden in the middle. It wasn't the best of Christmases for me, but was certainly memorable.

En route back to Bvde Thiers my friends all stopped outside the large prison. There was a big gap in the wall and I was told of a night of bombing which had been carried out some months earlier by the Allies. A direct attack on the wall had enabled some important British prisoners to escape, who might otherwise have been tortured to confess important secrets to their German captors.

We had been in Amiens for about three months and I wondered whether a delay in rejoining HQ in Brussels was entirely due to the rehabilitation of the railway system, or whether the Battle of the Bulge on the German border in December had anything to do with it. The latter had certainly been an unexpected turnaround for the Allies when the German army had forced back our frontline. Way back in Amiens, we could only speculate.

Paris fell on 25 August 1944. Le Général de Gaulle attended the service in Rouen Cathedral on Sunday 8 October 1944. I joined M. et Mme Médard for this on their special invitation, but not the dinner afterwards.

In the back garden of our
requisitioned house/office in Bvde
Thiers, Amiens.

With an officer and RSM in Amiens
in October 1944.

Right: Ghislain and her mother, who spoilt me with her oeufs à la neige.

Below: Grandmère Hélène M. Busseuil, me and Mme Busseuil at 66 Bvde Thiers, Amiens, in October 1944. My room in this household had been very recently vacated by a German.

Me with Ghislain Adam.

Me with a young friend, Josianne, whose
mother did my laundry on the banks of the
local canal.

An unlikely mascot.

Above left: Keeping warm in the bitterly cold winter and constant snowfalls.

Above right: An abandoned tank left by the wayside.

Another delay?
No 1 Team again, I expect!

(With apologies to Emett. JRG)

In Tn we had some clever draughtsmen. Our tea mugs were decorated for us individually. This is a Christmas card they drew while we were in Amiens.

M. Legrand (the Busseuils' neighbour) was an artist. This was one of his paintings I admired.

Amiens (Somme) Le Cirque – Pre-war entertainments were held here for our local troops.

Amiens – An old corner, pre-war, where the cobbles hurt my feet.

Amiens – This particular area was not one that I had time to visit.

Although my time was limited, I did manage to visit this ancient Cathedral.

The local canal in front of the Cathedral.

Another local view showing the dominant position of Amiens Cathedral.

5.– AMIENS (Somme)
La Cathédrale. L'Abside

Amiens Cathedral, showing the cobbled area, which was hard on military feet.

Chapter 8

On 7 February 1945 we were leaving Amiens; I was returning to HQ in Brussels and my 'lost tribe', the detachment, would be going on to Eindhoven and Nijmegen. I was sorry to be leaving them and the many friends I had made in Amiens. The men (in their words) said they would be losing their 'disturbing influence who kept away the blues', but this had been a two-way situation when they also had kept away mine. There were hugs and kisses as I said farewell to the Busseuils, even Grandmère who had been so fond of their earlier German lodger.

There was one tale I felt sure Monsieur would relate with relish in the coming years. It was the night I heard a rattling sound coming from my kitbag in the wardrobe. This had woken me up and it was a few minutes before it dawned on me it was a mouse, and then the whole household knew about it. This brave British member of the Liberation Army was jumping around on the bed squealing her head off. Madame, Grandmère, Berthe, could only look on in amazement, while Monsieur pretended not to understand what it was all about as I had no idea what was French for 'mouse'. Come to think about it, I still don't. I did not report this to my chaps across the road the next morning. I would never have heard the last of it.

We left the snow and slush behind early in the morning, crossing the border into Belgium at Valenciennes. We stopped at the railway station hoping to find a toilet. By now I was well used to 'making do' with whatever facility was available, which this time was a hole in the floor behind canvas on the platform. Fortunately the station was in great need of repair and deserted.

We arrived in Brussels late afternoon in pouring rain. My RE officers deposited me at the ATS office. I said goodbye not only to them, but to the Colonel's Humber, which had been very much more comfortable than the lorry or jeep. Inside the ATS office it was obvious I had not been expected, nor could any trace be found of my existence. There had been a complete change of the officers, and some of those who had previously been well known to me had, I think, returned to the UK.

At such short notice no billet was available for me and I was taken along to what had been an Embassy at 282 Rue de l'Abbaye, off the Avenue Louise, where a group of ATS girls were billeted. As it was a full house I was left with a bathroom as a temporary measure. This was the most luxurious bathroom I had ever seen, everything gold-plated, but at the end of the day, it was still a bathroom. A bedroom it was not.

That evening I put my army blanket in the bath and hoped for a good night's sleep. Unfortunately, no one had thought to tell me that electricity was being rationed in Brussels. The lights went out from late evening to eight in the morning, which left me completely in the dark without warning. I wasn't even sure where the door was. When I did find it I was able to enquire of some torch bearers as to where I could get something to eat. I was informed I would have to wait until morning when a lorry would call to take us to our mess and, by the way, this would also be in the dark at 7.30 a.m. And, they added, they hoped I would not be too disturbed as my temporary bedroom was their bathroom.

Feeling punch-drunk and a complete mess the following morning I spotted both Joyce and Jean at breakfast. Being the good friends they were they told me they had had a third spare bed in their billet, waiting for when I would be rejoining them, but had been told I would have to wait one more night.

In the meantime I was back with my original RSM Draper. Surprisingly, my typewriter and notebook were already on a desk in the room I would now be sharing with him and two very cheeky Belgian university students who were acting as interpreters. The Shell Mex building had been taken over by HQ. It was a treat to work there, it was all so normal. Even the working hours were more civilised, virtually 9 a.m. to 5 p.m.

I was now working for Brigadier Bell and his officer Major David Layton. The surprising thing about the Army was how easily one moved from one situation (and officers) to another. However, I was fortunate that from day one of my posting, way back in 1943, I was always in GHQ Home Forces/ HQ 21 Army Group; never posted from one unit to another. The Brigadiers changed, but below the rank of major they rarely did.

Our mess during the day was in an old army caserne (barracks) in a hilly part of the city. Walking there over cobbled streets played havoc with my feet, but there was an excellent tram service travelling back to the billets. Anyone prepared to hang on outside could travel free and, no doubt, at their peril.

The billet, where I now shared a room with my two friends, was also in the Avenue Louise (known as the avenue for the unemployed, i.e. millionaires). This particular apartment block, although not an old building, had been a Gestapo interrogation headquarters. It had a positively evil air about it and no one ventured down to the basement where one's imagination could run riot. The staircase walls were covered in smears which were extremely unpleasant to have to pass.

Meg Treadaway was an ATS officer who I came to know after the war through the introduction of another, namely Junior Commander Fraser-Tytler. Sadly Meg has died. When she stayed with me she told me she had accompanied Molly Gourlay (a famous golfer who had accompanied us when we left the UK for Normandy) to seek accommodation for three Companies who would be arriving in Brussels. Viewing this building in Avenue Louise, which had been the HQ for the German Gestapo, was pretty hair-raising for them. The Germans had departed in such haste everything had been left *in situ* – clothing, food and drink. I never asked her about the basement as I felt this was better unsaid.

Chapter 9

Brussels positively bustled with both British and American troops. The war was not yet over, but with occupied Europe now all but liberated, there was an air of 'any day now'. And so we waited in, what to me at any rate, was a luxurious existence. A weekly visit to the huge modern cinema, showing all the latest films; the Monty Club with its dance hall, café, hairdressers and music rooms, was all we could ask for. There was always this air of luxury wherever there were American troops behind the lines.

This was not entirely enjoyed by me. News from home was worrying. My family was still, in the sixth year, experiencing V2 raids over London. My elderly uncle, although retired, had insisted on doing his share of fire-watching duty, which had taken its toll on him. My sister Joan, expecting her baby was not at all well in her final weeks of waiting. She and my brother-in-law had moved in with our aunt and uncle when their flat had suffered bomb damage.

My parents were faring rather better in Sidcup, Kent, but as my aunt and uncle had been our guardians for many years, they were accepted as our next-of-kin. Early in April my ATS officer said she had received a telegram from the War Office asking for me to have a few days leave to attend my uncle's funeral. This was hurriedly arranged and I was put on an airplane to fly home. I had no time to worry about my very first flight. Right up until September 1939 planes were a rare sight, to be viewed from terra firma.

If there had been any seating accommodation in the Dakota it had been completely removed. The floor space was taken up by wounded military personnel, and I sat on the edge. I was very subdued both by the sight of these other passengers and the realisation I would never see my uncle again.

This was a short visit, returning home to south London, which I knew so well, but which for the present at least I was no part of. The air-raid sirens, so well known to me before leaving the UK, still wailed up and down at the approach of a raid. This time the groan of airplanes was replaced by a pulsating noise above, indicating the presence of a VI or V2, catapulted across the Channel, with no human pilot, only an engine that cut out above its target. The ensuing silence that followed was fearsome. There was a sigh of relief after its explosion, to know one was still alive, if only to await the next one.

There was a marked contrast between us in Brussels and my family enduring these constant air raids. It was a weird, unreal time. Here I was, attending my uncle's funeral, when so many had been killed around them. He had died a natural death, worn out by his nightly fire duties, as much a casualty of the war as any bomb victim.

I returned to Brussels in a sombre mood, leaving behind my aunt (Nan), now a widow, and my sister and brother-in-law who were awaiting the birth of their first baby. They were still enduring the V2s going over London. It had all affected me deeply.

At the end of April 1945 we received the wonderful news that some of us, who had left the UK way back in July 1944, were due for our first leave. Our instructions were to report to the Hotel Splendid at 0830 hours. On arrival at Croydon Airport we were to present ourselves to the Security Control and transport would be available to take us to the London District Transit Camp. Various documents had to be endorsed with the time and date on which to report back to cover onward and return journey (the rail travel section being only valid for travel to and from a seaport). On the return journey transport would be available to take us to Croydon from the LDTC (London District Transport Camp) in Gower Street. Departure from the airfield scheduled for 0800 hours, due to arrive 1000 hours.

While at home for these nine days I paid my sister a hurried visit, now in a basement ward (due to the continuing air raids) in King's College Hospital on Denmark Hill in London, as things were obviously not going as they should be for her. It was a totally unexpected surprise for both of us when our old school friend came in wearing her WAAF uniform. I had not seen her since we were all evacuated in 1939. Hopefully, we were able to cheer Joan up.

I flew back with my ticket from Croydon Airport, this time on a much smaller plane than the Dakota, with a few single seats on either side of the aisle. There was a box on each seat containing a sandwich and some fruit, and these small acts of generosity were enormously appreciated. It was a very bumpy ride. After first spiralling into the sky, my stomach seemed to be left behind as we appeared to drop down a mile or so with every bump. These first two flights were milestones in themselves, but for all the wrong reasons.

On my return to Brussels a second telegram from the War Office reported the sad news that my sister's baby had been born, but had died shortly after on 5 May. She had been christened and named Pamela (after my second name) in the hospital chapel. I was in no mood to celebrate VE day on 8 May 1945. On my way from Shell Mex I bought a newspaper, headlined 'La Guerre Est Finie!'. Brussels overflowed with British and American troops. They must have been collecting fire crackers for weeks. I went back to an empty billet.

The following Sunday I attended a service in a church packed to the rafters with mainly khaki uniforms. The GIs had a favourite hymn at that time – 'An Old Rugged Cross'. I just stood and listened to this mainly male congregation. The Belgian pastor gave a short sermon, alternating sentences in Flemish and English. La Guerre may have ended, but the opening up of the concentration camps, and the hundreds of parentless children from occupied countries, clearly indicated a massive task ahead.

The British HQ lost no time in establishing themselves in Bad Oeynhausen and that was where we would soon be heading. We were no longer BLA (British Liberation Army) but BAOR (British Army of the Rhine).

NAAFI/EFI - MONTGOMERY CLUB
SIGHTSEEING IN THE CITY OF BRUSSELS
arranged by WAGONS - LITS // COOK

BOOKINGS THROUGH W. V. S. AT INFORMATION BUREAU

Leaving the « **MONTGOMERY CLUB** », *we find on our way*
THE MEMORIAL *erected by the British Nation to the generous Belgians for their kindness to British wounded and prisoners 1914/18;*

THE LAW COURTS. *(Palais de Justice - 1879)* — constitutes the largest architectural creation of the 19 th Century. On september 3rd 1944, the Germans set fire to the building, and the dome fell in. The height of the dome was 104 m. (345 feet); by comparison the tower of the Town Hall could easily be placed in it.
On the way to Place Royale, on our right : the Synagogue - the Royal Academy of Music; on our left the Church of our Lady of the Victories of the Sablon *(N. D. des Victoires du Sablon)* one of the most remarkable specimens in Belgium of the third Gothic art. *(1304 but not completed until the sixteenth century.)* Opposite lies the Square du Petit Sablon. It consists of a garden enclosed by railings, the pillars of which are surmounted by 48 modern statuettes personifying the sixteenth-century guilds. The so-called Palais d'Egmont *(Montgomery Club) (1548 and rebuilt in the nineteenth century)* overlooks the square on the far side. On our left, Museum of Ancient Paintings, closed during the war.

PLACE ROYALE *(1777).* In the centre is a spirited equestrian statue by Simonis *(1848)* of Godfrey of Bouillon, leader of the First Crusade.
In front of us the Park of Brussels; turning to the right, the Place des Palais and the King's Palace ; further the Palais des Académies *(1826),* rue Ducale. Lord Byron in the spring

In February 1945 we left Amiens and headed for Brussels to rejoin the Tn officers there.

Botanical Gardens, Brussels. When we arrived in Brussels in February 1945 the civilian population was dwarfed by the troops, either stationed or on leave there. But sites, such as this one, were much in evidence.

Grand Place, Brussels. Here is the statue of the Manneken Pis. In contrast, I enjoyed watching the lace-makers in their front windows.

Above: A tramride from the billet in the Avenue Louise took us to the Shell Mex building where HQ had our offices.

Left: A photograph that I took, of some tram drivers enjoying their break.

View of Avenue Louis from our billet, previously a Gestapo HQ.

In a garden near our billet in Avenue Louise.

Brigardier Bell and other offiers, Shell Mex Offices, March 1945.

A lunch-hour break on the roof of Shell Mex
with my friend Jean and our Sergeant-Major
(RSM) in March 1945.

On Shell Mex roof with Jean and Adam.

Me, Margaret and Mollie enjoying the Monty Club in Brussels while waiting for the war to end.

ISSUE No. 6.

═BRUSSELS LEAVE═

SCHEME H

NAME...

YOUR HOTEL IS MARKED WITH A CROSS BELOW

	HOSTELS	MAP Ref.	Your Hostel
1	Plaza Hotel, Bvd Adolphe Max (EFI)	E.3	
2	Atlanta Hotel, Bvd Adolphe Max (Cdn Army)	E.4	
3	Hotel Gallia, Ave Marnix (RAF Officers only)	G.8	
4	Ancien Hotel Scheers, Bvd du Jardin Botanique (Ch Army)	F.3	
5	Hotel Cecil, Place Ch. Rogier (YMCA)	F.3	
6	Hotel des Colonies, Rue des Croisades (EFI)	F.2	
7	Albert Hotel, Place Ch. Rogier (YMCA)	F.3	
8	Hotel Ermitage, Bvd d'Ypres (Salvation Army)	C.2	
9	Hotel Sabot d'Or, Bvd d'Anvers (CWL)	C.2	
10	Hotel Splendid, Rue des Croisades (YWCA). Service Women only	F.2	✗
11	Hotel West End, Bvd d'Anvers (Ch. of Scotland)	E.2	
12	Toc H, 28/30 Bvd de Waterloo	F.9	
13	The Maple Leaf (Cdn Army) (Hotels Boulevards, Cosmopolite and Royal), Pl. Ch. Rogier	F.3	
14	The Maple Leaf Annexe (Cdn Army) (Hotels Monico, Rhin and Limbourg), Rue St. Lazare	F.2	

The above hotels are reserved exclusively for personnel of the Special 21 *Army Group Brussels. Leave Scheme.*

UNITED SERVICES WELFARE CENTRE, BRUSSELS GARRISON, is at 45 Boulevard Bischoffheim (corner of Rue Royale). Map Ref. G.4

NOTES

Do not talk about where your unit is or what it is. Do not discuss equipment, losses or battle experiences. The people of Brussels are very hospitable and will do all they can to make your leave enjoyable. Enjoy yourselves with them but do not tell them anything.

You are warned not to enter cafes unless a price list is displayed outside. Your accommodation and meals are free, but purchases from all canteens must be paid for in cash. You must not buy food in civilian restaurants. Haversack rations will be supplied for return journey to unit.

ISSUED BY ARMY WELFARE SERVICES AND EDUCATION BRANCH HQ BRUSSELS GARRISON

The notes on this page are of interest; the war was still being waged, albeit not for much longer.

30 Mar 1945

BRUSSELS.

Adolphe Max

THE MESSAGE OF

GOOD FRIDAY

Order of Service

CHORALE BELLIARD

Conductor: Monsieur Fritz Hoyois

BRUSSELS GARRISON LIGHT ORCHESTRA

Conductor: Sjt Mansel Thomas

Brussels, March 30th, 1945.

The singing of the choir and congregation at this service was wonderful. The short sermon was given, sentence by sentence, in English and Flemish/French.

The Good Friday service was held here, on 30 March 1945, for both English and American troops.

31 Mar 45
BRUSSELS

All Ranks Main and Rear Headquarters

I am circulating a message I have received from the Commander-in-Chief which should be brought to the notice of all ranks of both Main and Rear Headquarters. My reply is also circulated.

I would like to take this opportunity to say how grateful I am for the way all ranks have responded to the heavy demands that have been made upon them all. The Commander-in-Chief's message, and the way operations are going, are indeed fitting rewards for our efforts.

Main Headquarters,
21 Army Group.
30 Mar 45.

Major-General,
Chief of Staff.

Message received from Commander-in-Chief

I would like to express to you personally, and to all my staff that work under you, my great appreciation for the work that was done before we launched the Battle of the Rhine. I know well the amount of work that had to be done, and it had to be done in a short time. It could have been done in the time only by a first-class staff.

I always feel that at 21 Army Group we have the best staff in the world. Will you please let all the staff know how grateful I am.

B. L. Montgomery
Field-Marshal.

Tac HQ.
28 Mar 45.

Reply sent by Chief of Staff

To: Commander-in-Chief   30 Mar 45.
       (personal from Chief of Staff)

Your very kind message to the staff is greatly appreciated by us all. We hope to continue serving you to the limit of our ability until your great task is completed.

A short time after the German surrender near Lüneburg, we were flown into Germany to Bad Oeynhausen, not far from here, on 7 May 1945.

8 PC

Haven
Brussels

        The following message was issued by the Prime Minister to
troops of 21 Army Group this morning:-

"I REJOICE TO BE WITH THE CHIEF OF THE IMPERIAL GENERAL STAFF AT
FIELD MARSHAL MONTGOMERY'S HEADQUARTERS OF 21 ARMY GROUP DURING
THIS MEMORABLE BATTLE OF FORCING THE RHINE (.) BRITISH SOLDIERS -
IT WILL LONG BE TOLD HOW WITH OUR CANADIAN BROTHERS AND VALIANT
UNITED STATES ALLIES, THIS SUPERB TASK WAS ACCOMPLISHED (.) ONCE
THE RIVER LINE IS PIERCED AND THE CRUST OF GERMAN RESISTANCE IS
BROKEN DECISIVE VICTORY IN EUROPE WILL BE NEAR (.) MAY GOD PROSPER
OUR ARMS IN THIS NOBLE ADVENTURE AFTER OUR LONG STRUGGLE FOR KING
AND COUNTRY, FOR DEAR LIFE, AND FOR THE FREEDOM OF MANKIND (.)"

SIGNED - WINSTON S CHURCHILL PRIME MINISTER AND MINISTER OF DEFENCE.

Distribution: All Branches   IMMEDIATE
                Main and Rear

These messages from General Montgomery and Eisenhower gave a boost to all who had experienced the long years of the war. There was still no VE Day to celebrate, but the end was becoming inevitable.

SUPREME HEADQUARTERS
ALLIED EXPEDITIONARY FORCE

TO ALL MEMBERS OF THE ALLIED EXPEDITIONARY FORCE:

The task which we set ourselves is finished, and the time has come for me to relinquish Combined Command.

In the name of the United States and the British Common-wealth, from whom my authority is derived, I should like to convey to you the gratitude and admiration of our two nations for the manner in which you have responded to every demand that has been made upon you. At times, conditions have been hard and the tasks to be performed arduous. No praise is too high for the manner in which you have surmounted every obstacle.

I should like, also, to add my own personal word of thanks to each one of you for the part you have played, and the contribution you have made to our joint victory.

Now that you are about to pass to other spheres of activity, I say Good-bye to you and wish you Good Luck and God-Speed.

Dwight Eisenhower

A VE Day message from Dwight Eisenhower.

Montgomery's caravan was where he lived and worked once he was abroad. In London, prior to D-Day, he was based in St Paul's School, Hammersmith.

AND SO THEY LOST THEIR ADMIRAL

As Admiral Siegfried Engel, O.C. the German naval base at Buxtehude, Hamburg, left as a prisoner of the British, German Wrens, queueing-up for a meal, waved "Good-bye."

A passenger on
my plane over to
the UK.

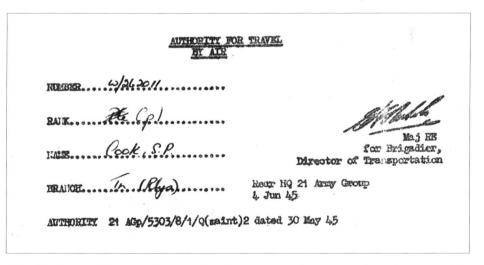

AUTHORITY FOR TRAVEL
BY AIR

NUMBER...... W/242011..............

RANK........ Pte (Cpl)..............

NAME........ Cook, S.P. ....

BRANCH........ Tr (Rlys)..........

AUTHORITY   21 AGp/5303/8/1/Q(maint)2 dated 30 May 45

Maj RE
for Brigadier,
Director of Transportation
Rear HQ 21 Army Group
4 Jun 45

After VE Day, my first leave for a week at home for nearly a year, and my first taste of air travel. Also, the time of my long-awaited promotion.

N.C.(s' RESPONSIBILITIES.

WHY ARE N.C.Os. NECESSARY?
　　To ensure maximum efficiency by:-
　　(1) Good leadership.
　　(2) Care of the private so that she is physically and mentally
　　　　fit.

WHAT ARE YOUR RESPONSIBILITIES?
(1) To the private
　　(a) Leadership:-　　(i)　To have a knowledge and understanding of
　　　　　　　　　　　　　　　each individual in your charge.
　　　　　　　　　　(ii)　To gain their trust and respect by fair
　　　　　　　　　　　　　dealing, by fighting for their rights
　　　　　　　　　　　　　and privileges, and by setting a high
　　　　　　　　　　　　　standard both for yourself and for them
　　　　　　　　　　(iii)　To inspire them to give of their best, at
　　　　　　　　　　　　　all times.
　　　　　　　　　　(iv)　To watch for, and train, future N.C.Os
　　(b) Knowledge:-　　(i)　To know their rights and privileges and
　　　　　　　　　　　　　how to set about getting them.
　　　　　　　　　　(ii)　To understand the circumstances and
　　　　　　　　　　　　　difficulties of their work.
　　　　　　　　　　(iii)　To understand your position as an N.C.Os
　　(c) Teamwork:-　　(i)　To make them realise you are all working
　　　　　　　　　　　　　together for the same purpose.
　　　　　　　　　　(ii)　To know, and make full use, of each
　　　　　　　　　　　　　member of your team.
　　　　　　　　　　(iii)　To instill esprit-de-corps and loyalty.
(2) To your fellow N.C.Os.
　　(a) Realisation of your common purpose - the well being of the
　　　　privates.
　　(b) Loyalty to each other.
　　(c) Training of your junior N.C.Os for further promotion.
(3) To your Officers.
　　(a) Loyalty and backing.
　　(b) Maintenance of close liaison between the privates and their
　　　　officers.
　　(c) Efficiency.
(4) To your Country.
　　(a) Whole-hearted service as a member of the British people in
　　　　the National Emergency.
　　(b) Example, as a member of H.M.Forces.
　　(c) Efficiency, as a paid servant of the public.
Promotion is not an award for efficient service; it is a compliment
to your ability to take greater responsibility for others. The fact
that you have the ability to lead, will have been proved before you
were promoted; it is for you to satisfy yourself and your Officers,
that you are giving the very best of which you are capable.

Discipline, Esprit-de-Corps and Morale.
　　Discipline - the ingrained habit of cheerful and willing
　　　　　　　　　　　　　　　　　　　　　　　obedience.
　　Esprit-de-Corps - the spirit of the Service; that which gives
　　　　　　　　　　　　　　　　　　　　　　　　　life.
　　Morale - The TONE of a body of people: control of conduct by
　　　　　　　　　　　　　　　　　　intelligence and understanding.
1. Discipline.
　　"Goodwill and voluntary subjection of the individual inclination
in pursuit of a commond end."
　　Essential to ensure all round efficiency by co-ordinated action
however separated the individuals; singleness of purpose; the carrying out of the Commander's intention, whether she is present or not;
the smooth running of a community - the basis is self-discipline
and unselfishness.
　　Obtained through Drill, clear explanation and giving of orders
and good leadership.
Esprit-de-Corps. Knowledge of, and pride, in, our own Service;
realisation of the importance of each individual in the general scheme.

INSTR FOR PERSONNEL OF WOMENS' SERVICES PROCEEDING
ON AND RETURNING FROM LEAVE BY AIR

OUTWARD

1. You will proceed to the Hotel Splendid/~~Town Major/remain at the Q(Mov)Air Office, 55 Cantersteen.~~
    Currency will be exchanged at the Hotel Splendid.

2. **TRANSPORT**
    Transport will convey you to the Airport and will depart Hotel Splendid 0830 hrs.

3. **AT THE DEPARTURE AIRPORT**
    Report to the Movement Control Offr, handing him the pro-forma at the head of this instruction, which you will complete and detach before arrival at the airport, together with Part 2 of your AF W3145C or D and your Air Travel Ticket. He will instruct you as to arrangements for your emplanement.

4. **TRANSPORT - CROYDON - LONDON**
    On arrival at CROYDON report to RAF Passenger and Freight Section for Security Control and Customs Regulations. Transport will be available to take you to the London District Transit Camp, Gower Street, from where you will be dispersed to your leave destination.

5. **DURATION OF LEAVE**
    (a) The period of leave in UK will be nine days from day of arrival in UK, both days inclusive, excepting those proceeding to SCOTLAND, NORTHERN IRELAND, EIRE, SHETLANDS, ORKNEYS and other Islands (except ISLE of WIGHT). .... W3145 .... For record purposes present your AF W3145C or D to the Adjt of the Transit Camp to have it endorsed with the time and date on which you are to report back there. It is there that Sections 3, 4 and 5 of AF W3145C or D will be exchanged for AF W4098 or 4099, to cover onward and return journey (the rail travel section of AF W3145C or D being only valid for travel to and from a seaport) except for those proceeding to NORTHERN IRELAND, EIRE or ISLE of MAN, to whom Railway Warrants (AB422A) will be issued.

    (b) If for any reason shown on the cover of AF W3145C or D you are granted an extension of leave, you will ensure that London District Transit Camp is informed of the date on which you will be returning to this theatre by air.

RETURN

6. **TRANSPORT - LONDON to CROYDON**
    Transport will be available to take you to CROYDON from LDTC.

7. **DEPARTURE FROM AIRFIELD**
    Is scheduled for 0800 hrs which means you are due to arrive in BRUSSELS at 1000 hrs.

8. **ARRIVAL IN BRUSSELS**
    Transport will convey you from the airfield to the Hotel Splendid where

INSTRUCTIONS

1. (a) Passengers will report to ARMY MOVEMENT CONTROL 92 FSP R.A.F. B151 Airfield BUCKEBURG, map reference W919097.

   (b) Passengers proceeding to airfield by shuttle service from this HQ will report to Q(M)Air, 35 Herforder Strasse 1¾ hrs prior to scheduled time of take off.

   (c) Passengers proceeding to airfield by own transport will report as in 1(a) above 45 mins before scheduled time of take off. Passengers who report less than 45 mins before take off will not be allowed on the a/c.

2. RETURN BOOKINGS

   (a) UK   On departure from BAOR passengers will carry with them RAF Form No. 2768 completed in duplicate and sponsored by head of Branch or Service. These forms will be submitted to War Office, Q(M)8c, as soon as possible either in person or by messenger. Telephone reservations cannot be made.

   (b) CONTINENTAL Passengers will carry RAF Form No. 2768 completed in triplicate and sponsored by head of Branch or Service. These will be submitted to appropriate Booking Office for return reservations.

3. AIR BOOKING OFFICES

   (a) HQ BAOR   - Q(M)Air, Central Booking Office, 35 Herforder Strasse. (Tel HQ BAOR ext 3034 & 3035)

   (b) BRUSSELS (B56) - Air Traffic Office, Grand Hotel, Boulevard Anspach, (Tel Brussels Trunks direct, Brussels local 103)

   (c) COPENHAGEN (B160) - Air Traffic Office, Ground Floor of DAGMARHUS, RAADHUSPLADSEN, COPENHAGEN.

   (d) VALKENBURG (B93) - Air Traffic Office, 33 Platts Den Haag, THE HAGUE
   (e) ISERLOHN   - Q(M) 1 Corps HQ Booking Office (Tel HQ 1 Corps Dist. ext 34)

   (f) HAMBURG (B168) - Air Traffic Office, Cunard House, 4 Colannaden, HAMBURG (Tel HAMBURG Trunks 352124 and 352136)

   (g) UK   - War Office, Q(M) 8c, Room 15, QMG House, 10, Whitehall Place, SW1 (Tel War Office 1570 & 992)

   (h) PARIS (A54)   - Brit Army Staff, 62 Rue Faubourg St Honore, (Tel ANJOU840 ext 103)

   (j) BERLIN/GATOW - Q(M) Central Booking Office, 43 Ringstrasse, (Tel HQ British Tps BERLIN ext 5618)

   (k) FRANKFURT (Y74) - Booking Office, HQ USFET (Tel ROUNDUP Ext 24800)

4. Passengers are warned that censorship regulations prohibit the carrying of mail out of the theatre.

5. Baggage will be restricted to 65lbs per passenger on DAKOTA services.   "   "   "   "   " 25lbs "   "   " ANSON "

ARMY BOOK X 802

Surname .... *Cook* ....

Initials .... *S.P.* ....

Army No. .... *W/262011* ....

A.T.S. AND V.A.D.
RELEASE BOOK

CLASS "A"

Any person finding this Book is requested to hand it in to any Barracks, Post Office, or Police Station, for transmission to the Under Secretary of State, The War Office, London, S.W.I.

CLOTHING COUPONS & RATION BOOK

These are NOT issued by the Dispersal Unit. They may be obtained by presenting your Release Book at the Local Food Office.

This book must be presented at the Post Office whenever you cash a postal draft or one of the drafts in your payment book, to enable the Post Office Official to record the date of payment on the inside page of the front cover.

51-5238

Chapter 10

We boarded a plane taking us to Minden where we would be joining a convoy to Bad Oeynhausen. I now had a collection of booklets of 'Dos & Don'ts': one for France, one for Belgium and one for Germany. In the latter fraternisation was strictly forbidden. Strangely enough I do not think I had envisaged mixing with any Germans. The barrier had existed for six long years and it would take time to realise there was now the possibility we could all work together for peace.

We were at the rear end of a long convoy of lorries. At that time, motorways were unknown to us in the UK. Where we had left behind narrow winding lanes connecting one village to another, and just two-way roads for traffic in towns, the sight of our first autobahn was something to behold – long and straight and very wide. The farms were neat and clean. Women in long black dresses and headgear, as seen in medieval times, were working in some of the fields. They may, of course, have been from a local nunnery. If we were the first view they had of the British army, they may have had thumping hearts as to what to expect as our whole convoy came to a halt. We had been travelling for quite some time when word was passed down the line we needed to make ourselves comfortable. In the heart of the German countryside, men dropped out of their lorries to one side and we females to the other. Returning to our vehicles we departed. I am not sure our onlookers would have approved.

It was all so peaceful with no sign of the ravaged countryside I had seen in France. Bad Oeynhausen was one of the German spas, where one could see signs of no expense having been spared to provide for the privileged. Joyce and I were billeted in one of four apartments. We were on the ground floor and discovered we had only to open our window, put our hands out and pick fruit from a tree. I found it rather touching that the previous owners had left much of their furniture behind and some personal items, such as knitted egg cosies and even correspondence. Although, while in Brussels, I had been given some pages of German to copy, I had no idea what it was as I do not understand the language. And so it was when I found some letters and a postcard. I did, however, see 'Heil Hitler' written after the signature. Maybe that had been obligatory.

ATS girls were still being posted into HQ. My other friend, Jean, had been posted to Bielefeld, not too unhappy to leave us as her fiancé, Adam, had also been posted there. Joyce and I now shared our room with Margaret, a delightful Scottish girl with our sense of fun. Materially we were very comfortable and sat out on the lawn after work in the hot sunny weather. We were even allowed to shed our jackets, roll up our shirtsleeves and abandon our ties. We had access to the local spa baths where we could sit in the round wooden tubs and soak ourselves clean.

There was, however, an air of abnormality in the office. Our cleaners, no longer sappers, were German schoolteachers or professionals, looking for some kind of employment. With the 'no fraternisation' rule it was an unnatural environment for all of us.

The civilian Control Commission was moving in to take over. After our army issue of khaki uniforms, shapeless underwear and flat-heeled shoes, we found it amusing to see our female replacements arriving with their suitcases containing very feminine wardrobes, fur coats, etc. It was all an anticlimax. Work had slowed down to (as far as I was concerned) boring. I was now working for Sir Robert Marriott who was in the Control Commission, but I was still with RSM Draper who had first steered me through all those fish nuts and fish bolts, when I had been posted into 21 Army Group in 1943.

I tried my hand at some tapestry work with highly coloured wools, with no more success than when I started it in Amiens. 'Looks as though a bomb has hit it', was the general comment. Well, at least it was a topical theme.

I was even more bored when a high temperature and extreme tiredness landed me in the small Sick Bay. I just lay on the bed in an otherwise empty room while my temperature was taken morning and evening. After a few days it was declared I was obviously someone whose temperature was normally high, so I was transferred back to my billet. Without reporting this before, I had experienced something similar while in Brussels.

News from home was a constant worry. My sister was far from fully recovered, and she and her husband were considering moving to Ilford in Essex where he was working. This would leave my aunt to cope alone. Some light relief came my way when I heard my 'lost tribe' had moved from Nijmegen to Lustringen, south of Bad Oeynhausen. RSM Draper arranged for him, Joyce and me to be granted a loan of Major David Layton's Land Rover and his driver one Saturday, to take us down to see them. Not only did we thoroughly enjoy this visit, we were also outside the restricted area where we were 'fenced in' in those early days.

The driver pointed out to us a small mountain that we passed on the way, rumoured as having been dug out below to house a munitions factory, operated by prisoners of war from the occupied countries. I recall seeing a film after the war about a similar factory below a hill, but whether this was fictional or true I do not know.

Our billet in Bad Oeynhausen; a beautiful area but sealed off from the civilian population. A pass was necessary, with an armed escort, until the non-fraternisation rule was relaxed.

Another view of our billet in Bad Oeynhausen.

Tongue hanging out – I do not think I fully approved of the photographer.

Outside the perimeter we had a pass to tour the surrounding area. Rumour had it that this was the hill hollowed out for a factory, with a workforce of captured men from the occupied countries.

Right: Me, Joyce and Margaret in the summer of 1945 in Germany.

Below: Before the arrival of the Control Commission, who would be taking over, we spent the long, hot summer with more relaxed rules, allowed to leave jackets off, remove ties, roll up our sleeves.

A German bank note at the time.

Chapter 11

In the weeks before Christmas 1945, demobilisation was being looked forward to, but during July/August we were being given our first full leave of two weeks. As it happened, my leave coincided with Jean's, not Joyce's. As she was now in Bielefeld we met up at the railway station in Luneberg, as we were travelling by train. This was to be a longer journey than we had anticipated as our first stop was not at a station but at a railway bridge across the Rhine, which had just been blown up. This entailed a difficult diversion, as it was no doubt intended to be by the perpetrators.

At some stage we decided our skirts were getting badly creased, sitting in them for such a long period, so we took them off. There was no one else in our carriage. Gradually we dozed off as we had started out early that morning. We were finally woken up just after midnight, very thirsty and hungry. We found we had stopped in the main railway station in Brussels, and were about to leave. Outside the train we saw a trolley of food and drink. We both stood up, opened the window and yelled out for them to come outside our carriage. Imagine the amusement when the trolley owner found two skirt-less ATS girls standing up in full view of passengers on the platform. We happily waved them all goodbye and sat down to eat and drink for the rest of the journey to the coast.

In the early hours we caught a boat across to Dover, and then another train to Victoria, where we spent some time making ourselves presentable before going on to our respective homes. These two weeks had been looked forward to, but they gave me little pleasure. My sister was still recovering from the loss of her baby and she and my brother-in-law had moved to North London. My uncle had died and Nan, who had survived six years of the war, was now alone. Nothing was the same.

Neither Joyce nor I were among the early ones to be demobilised, but due to the change in my circumstances at home it was decided to post me back to London. I would have preferred to be demobilised; having been only with HQ I was never going to settle in an ATS unit at this late stage. I had to accept that at least I would be nearer home.

My air ticket flew me back to London Airport, unrecognisable now as Heathrow. Planes came down on what was virtually a field, cordoned off by a low wire fence which could be easily climbed over. I was being posted to a unit in Paddington and billeted in Sussex Gardens, my room being at the top of a three- or four-storey house. It was very bleak after our billet in Bad Oeynhausen.

I was never quite sure what this particular unit did. Being given the week's menus to type, I waited for some dictation or typing. The other girls, all clerks, appeared to have plenty to do while I sat feeling like a fish out of water. It was the first time I felt completely out of control of my situation.

As I had grown used to in Germany, I relaxed at my typewriter with my jacket unbuttoned. This was, of course, unforgiveable, but the Sergeant in charge of this office took obvious delight in reporting my lapse direct to the CO instead of asking me to keep to the rules. Fortunately, the officer was far more interested in my army career and medal ribbons, saying she could not understand why I was still only a Corporal and would be recommending me for promotion. This sounded favourable news, but in actual fact I had never wanted to be a Sergeant or take on a Sergeant's responsibilities. However, I wasn't going to argue as more money at this late stage would be welcome, particularly as I anticipated having to be the breadwinner once I returned home.

There just wasn't enough for me to do. What little I was given I finished too quickly, so when the officer heard there was a vacancy over at Wellington Barracks for a shorthand typist, I was sent to fill it. For two reasons this was not a success. I entered the gates and was halfway across the parade ground when I was deafened by a voice of thunder. I was to learn no one, absolutely no one of my rank was allowed to cross this hallowed ground. Did I walk back or walk on? Keeping a straight back and looking firmly ahead I walked on. The second reason this appointment did not last long was that I was taking dictation from a Welsh officer who was completely indecipherable to me. I should have known what I was in for when I entered the Welsh Barracks. He probably did not understand me either.

I was beginning to feel like a crazy mixed-up kid, but was pleased to hear I was now an Acting Sergeant until my promotion was confirmed. The responsibility of having to check in late passes at night did not rest easily on my shoulders, as I knew it wouldn't. My ability was to take dictation, type at high speeds and be accurate, but responsibility in any other sphere was not for me. I have always liked to make my own decisions. Even on the typewriter I really enjoyed matching up four sheets of brief-size paper with columns of figures all having to marry up. A computer would have taken away the satisfaction of doing it myself. The officer back at the Paddington office was not going to give up, and this time I did not let her down.

It was now the Spring of 1946 and I was nearly twenty-three. Both Joyce and Jean had been demobilised and were back in 'civvy street' job hunting. Both had enlisted after me, so why was I being overlooked? My ATS officer decided to look into this for me and found my records were not 'where they should have been'. This was not exactly a surprise. I had left Bayeux and not received any pay until I had been in Amiens for some time, so it would not have been surprising to learn there was no record of my whereabouts at all. This was confirmed after I left the Army (see pages 20–23).

However, I was now being sent over to an office close to the Albert Hall presided over by Sir Marcus Lipton, the MP for Brixton. He was an army officer dealing with military divorce cases. He was being kept extremely busy at a time when so many men were returning home after husbands and wives had lived so far apart and for so long. There was a great deal of very sad reading, all sensitively dealt with by Sir Marcus. Quite by chance, the other secretary was a civilian, a Miss Fitzpatrick, with whom my sister had worked in Rotunda under Whitehall in 1942. I enjoyed working with her and Sir Marcus. I also enjoyed the walk every morning across Hyde Park.

In September 1946 I was asked to attend a medical at the Millbank Military Hospital as I had served abroad and this was a necessity before I could be released. It was nearly a year since leaving Germany and it had been unsettling to hear from Joyce and Jean that they were now well and truly back in civilian life. The following year both were getting married. Being posted back to London was not entirely the answer to my aunt's situation, although I was able to see her at weekends.

I was not therefore, pleased to hear from the Medical Officer that he was not happy about 'something', and wanted me to have a more thorough investigation. I had a urine test and, yes, I did tire easily; something I had become aware of way back in Brussels. I had also had a temperature and a few days off in Germany.

There was, however, a big 'but' to a more thorough investigation – I would have to remain in the Army. In the circumstances I could not agree to this. This was my decision and never something I regretted later as I would not have had my two sons. After the birth of the second one in the 1950s, my GP sent me to see a Consultant, which resulted in an 'all action' situation. I had a long-term left kidney disease, which had spread to a fallopian tube and an ovary, necessitating an urgent nephrectomy, and, after a good recovery gap, a complete hysterectomy. The wonderful long-term care I received at Epsom Hospital in Surrey and the fact I have always been teetotal resulted in the following years being ones of full activity in a happy marriage.

Chapter 12

The six years of war left every individual with memories and experiences never to be forgotten. The First World War left my father with memories he preferred to forget. He never did, he just buried them. The fact he was awarded the Military Medal for action in Ypres would testify to this. When I returned home I heard for the first time that he had also been in the Battle of the Somme, but how very different were our memories of France and Belgium. Every fighting man in the 1914–18 war had been in my estimation 'big cogs'. In comparison, I had been a very 'small cog', but both of us had given our best.

Both my aunt and I had difficulty in settling down. The war had been long and wearing for her and we were still rationed for most things. I was restless, missing being with a large group of colleagues, and I had no idea which field I wanted to go ahead in. Two of the officers I had known in 21 Army Group recommended me for the Foreign Office, but for every promotion there were exams, which did not appeal to me. Gordon and Gotch, with whom I had been in 1941/42, had a vacancy for me, but I turned that down. And then I heard of an entirely new avenue. The work would probably not be taxing enough for me, but the salary was enticing.

My interview was with a partner in a small company in Mayfair, London, but big in Property Maintenance and Auctioneers: Jones Lang Wootton & Sons. This particular partner was the property auctioneer. He greeted me with 'I suppose I should dictate something for you to type back.' He sounded so unenthusiastic that I suggested I work for him for a month, and if I didn't suit him or the work didn't suit me, we part company. He accepted this with relief, and I was still there as a private secretary until I married in 1951. Even then, after giving in my notice, my mother-in-law received a telephone message while we were on honeymoon: 'Would I consider going back?' I did, on the agreement that I started half an hour later and finished half an hour earlier. They were happy days. The excellent salary and good bonus at Christmas was very useful when starting out on married life.

Way back in my young days I had been a Brownie and my Tawny Owl had a young brother. His days in the Fleet Air Arm and mine in the Army had broken the days when we knew each other in the Guides and Boys' Brigade and other church activities. Meeting up again after demobilisation, we married and had nearly forty years together. Sadly, he died twenty years ago of cancer. And here I am, still going strong. My busy fingers are no longer employed on my ancient, but still very efficient typewriter; I have at last relented and parted from it. This is through no fault of my fingers, still very agile, but I have returned to an even more ancient piece of equipment – a pen. We go along more comfortably together.

Chapter 13

My husband was, eventually, a Fellow in each of the Institutes of Civil, Mechanical and Water Engineers. I was able to attend world conferences with him when he was often one of the main speakers. There was only one place I was not anxious to go to and that was Berlin. However, he was so keen for me to overcome my still deep emotions about the Holocaust in Germany that I reluctantly agreed to go. Our flight had to land at Hanover before we could continue on to Berlin as we would be flying over the Russian zone. The first morning, after my husband had signed on at the Conference centre, we decided to have a walk round. My earlier memories of Germany were soon dissipated when we saw Marks & Spencer, C&A and other stores; we could have been in Oxford Street.

We had been walking for some time and on our way back decided to take a taxi. We gave the driver the name of our hotel to which he said 'Nein.' My husband believed all foreigners should speak English; if they appeared not to understand he would say it again louder. Still the driver shook his head saying 'Nein.' I began to feel World War Three was about to start when the taxi driver relented and we got in. He drove round the corner and we all collapsed in laughter. Without realising it our walk had completed a circle and there was our hotel.

We always took our car in the early days and our favourite country was Switzerland where my husband had many business colleagues. He would arrange trips there during our sons' school holidays at Easter from the time the younger one was four and the older one seven. We drove from Surrey to Dover, took the ferry across the Channel, and then drove down through France or Germany. Over the years we always chose a different route, making it as interesting as possible, staying one night in an out-of-the-way town or village.

In the early sixties, I not only packed for the boys and me, but my husband's evening suits. I only once forgot an important item and this was his collar studs. While my husband was at a business meeting, the boys and I spent the day trying to find a shop in Schaffhausen where I could purchase these studs. No matter how I tried to explain what I wanted no one understood. They spoke only Swiss-German or a patois of their own.

Eventually, when I had all but given up, I found them. I asked the assistant if he would write down the word 'stud' for me. This four letter word transcribed into a positive alphabet, much to our amusement.

We travelled to various points of France, including Paris, but although I never went to Rouen again we did spend a night in Amiens. Madame Busseuil had died, but Monsieur was able to meet my family. He did mention the 'night of the fire' when I was there in 1944, but I could not recall it as it was in the town centre I believe. We went to Luxembourg, Liechenstein, into Austria, Winterthur and Schaffhausen and Lake Constance in Switzerland, and later on, Geneva and Zurich.

Once our sons were over twenty my husband and I took our car over to Denmark to drive into Sweden where we attended a conference at Jonkoping. Hungary was memorable. It was still under a Communist regime and we were the only two from a western country at a conference attended by delegates from all over Eastern Europe.

One of the world conferences for water engineers was held in London and we stayed at the Royal Garden Hotel in Knightsbridge. Also staying there was a member of a foreign government with his family. His wife introduced me to their two children who told me they were having a lovely time. They were in a suite of rooms and they had brought their roller skates! Well, it obviously kept them occupied, but I would never have allowed my sons to use a hotel for such a purpose. While in Liechenstein they had played with their small cars, some of which found their way under the heavy German furniture and are probably still there.

Chapter 14

I have never been a tourist, but wherever we went I loved to meet people from all over the world. I have never been to America, but have met many Americans. Their wives would discuss my husband's hobby of embroidered tapestry, particularly when they heard he sketched the picture onto the canvas before working it. Once he drew in detail the four-storey high triple expansion steam engine at Kempton Park and then worked on a fine canvas, which he donated to the Institution of Civil Engineers in London and is still there. Sir Hugh Casson, when he saw it being framed at the Royal Academy, praised it highly. As Laurie was a member of the Embroiderers' Guild at Hampton Court I was left among the husbands while he chatted away with the wives. I greatly appreciate all the arts (traditional) but have never been gifted in any. My two sisters were very accomplished pianists, but I could never master two hands doing their own thing. Once I had a typewriter however, I was well away.

My widowed years have been spent getting to know Wales and the Welsh and I would never move away from here now. I love the country and I have to say, this 'foreigner' has become very much at home here.

* * *

And so to the last of the four generations of women I have taken, to indicate how very different my own life has been from that of my grandmother's, my mother's and my elderly aunt's, covering the past 150 years. Two World

Wars, it has to be admitted, created an emancipated world for women, when they were called upon to carry out duties virtually unacceptable before, or at least treated with greater respect. In today's world many wives are the breadwinners, even running their own businesses. I am not sure whether this is a step too far with children missing the motherly role in the home. One thing is for certain; my forebears would have appreciated their steaming Monday morning coppers being replaced by a washing machine, iron-free shirts and central heating, a holiday abroad, meals cooked in minutes in a microwave. I do wonder, however, whether it is in the nature of women to seek to be appreciated in whatever role they play, and women certainly played their part in two World Wars.

Tn History

Until the middle of August there was no great change in the activities of the Tn service. Traffic continued to go across the beaches through Mulberry and the small ports in the beach head and preparations for the expected advance north continued. But when the final breakthrough to the Seine did take place and this was followed by a helter-skelter advance through France and Belgium into Holland, the whole picture changed completely. Tn was brought up against two really big problems; firstly, how to organise a long rail L of C from the RMA across the Seine right forward into Holland, and secondly, the problem of opening the Channel ports to shorten the L of C and to bring supplies by a shorter route through ports that would be able to operate right through the winter. By the end of September both these tasks had been successfully tackled and there was a rail L of C of somewhat meagre capacity from the RMA right through to Eindhoven and the port of Dieppe was open and the ports of Ostend, Boulogne and Antwerp were being made ready to accept shipping.

The development of the rail L of C focused from the very start on the development of Caen, which had to become the main traffic and locomotive sector in spite of the damage that had been sustained there. Energetic action had to be taken to repair yards, sidings, workshops and locomotive sheds, communications and signals. This was followed, as soon as the line advanced, by concentration on opening railway line to Serquigny and to the Seine and later Railway Construction troops were spread out all along the

line to Serqueux and forward into Belgium. For this four Rly Construction &
Maintenance Groups and fourteen Rly Construction coys had been brought
over into the beach head in readiness.

Throughout north-eastern France bomb damage at rail centres had been
extensive and this damage had been combined with serious demolition
south of the Seine and more spasmodic demolitions where the advance had
become very rapid. Some hundreds of bridges were down in the British Zone
in France and the damage to installations and track was heavy.

The problem, from a 21 Army Group point of view, was a dual one. In the
first place the most profitable route for repair had to be selected and in the
second place the actual work of repair had to be organised utilising British
resources in manpower and whatever assistance could be obtained from the
French and Belgians.

The first part of the problem involved the use of any wide-range
reconnaissance and it was found extremely difficult to control and coordinate
the activities of these reconnaissance parties owing to the extremely bad
system of communications and an acute shortage of transport.

It was decided, owing to the construction of all bridges across the Seine,
to establish railheads south of the river with a rail link across the river and
rail trails somewhere north of the river. This system was satisfactory and
closed the gap until the Seine bridge at Le Manoir was completed on 22
September. Two main bridges were down also across the Somme, but it was
found possible to bypass this damage by a diversion at Doullens. Apart from
this in the north-eastern area, it was possible to get the L of C completed
right through to Brussels with the exception of a major bridging job at Hal.

It was, however, soon discovered that it was one thing to repair a line
and provide a through track, but quite another to work heavy traffic over
it immediately and it was not until the end of September that the railways
of France and Belgium began to show signs of settling down to provide
a long and reliable service, and even by that date it by no means worked
smoothly. The Railway Operating organisation had to tackle this problem.
Communications were very bad, particularly in the Amiens Arrondissement.

They were inadequate and unreliable, but after superhuman efforts
involving very close collaboration with the SNCF and the SNCB, the main
trunk links that had to control the circuits were nearly completed by the
Railway Signals staff by the end of September.

The operating service were short of stock and locomotives due to the inadequate allocation of stock and locomotives, which were being imported through Cherbourg, but this problem gradually straightened itself out by the end of September. The opening of the Dieppe train ferry on 29 September settled the problem of locomotives once and for all.

Amongst the most awkward of problems was that of coal, all of which was being imported from the UK via Caen and Cherbourg, but the coal traffic required for moving trains north of the Seine was taking up paths across the Seine that could ill be spared. Every effort was being made towards the end of September to arrange for coal to be provided from French sources in the mining area of the north.

To tackle the problem of organising a rail L of C which was operated entirely by British troops on some sectors, half and half by French and British on another and entirely French or Belgian on a third, a Corps flexibility of organisation was essential. It was found necessary by mid-September to drop the standard Railway Operating Group and Railway Unit organisation in the area south of the Seine and to set up a Divisional Superintendent's office under the commanding officer of 3 Rly Op Gp at Caen. At the same time the head of the Railways Branch left Bayeux, where 21 Army Group remained, and went forward to Rouen where it could maintain some contact with TRANCO. Rouen was first selected as the base from which to send out the necessary railway construction reconnaissance. It was also suitable for the central control of Railway Operating. Nevertheless it was soon found that it was necessary to have a Railway Operating headquarters further forward and in addition to AD Tn (Rly Op), who was with TRANCO, 7 Rly Op Gp had moved forward to Amiens. As soon as Brussels fell the AD Tn (Rly Op) who had been with TRANCO set up his office alongside the SNCB.

In the area south of the Seine the actual operating itself was completed and finished but at times it was not possible to attain the agreed programme. The following are some of the particular reasons for this. Firstly, a spate of rail breaks between Caen and Mezidon which were due to the effects of shelling. Secondly, accentuation of traffic working difficulties by engine failures and off axle boxes, particularly on the US double-headed through trains. Thirdly, there was congestion in the Caen Yard in the RMA area due to limited siding capacity, loading points and depots. Fourthly, there was a shortage of engine power particularly not sufficient numbers of British locomotives and insufficient shed facilities to handle locomotives at Caen. Fifthly, we were trying to tackle the problem with inexperienced Railway Operating troops over a very difficult section of line and they required time to settle down.

On the other hand, north of the Seine apart from the problem of water and repair of lines, the greatest difficulty encountered was that of reorganising the Operating service in collaboration with the French and later with the Belgians. Though the operating units were quite capable of being used to some extent for this type of railway operating, they were definitely not ideal for the job as they did not contain enough NCOs and officers and had grossly inadequate quantities of transport.

The second half of the problem on the Tn side was that of opening up the Channel ports as quickly as possible and thus relieving the strain on the L of C from the RMA. It was not possible to open up Caen as a port until the end of August, but other facilities were found to be adequate and work continued on the winterisation of Mulberry in case inadequate port facilities were captured to the north. In order to open up these Channel ports, everything depended on planning ahead and preparations were made well in advance to tackle each of the ports as they were captured. Reconnaissance parties were sent forward together with Royal Naval parties, the Port Commandant and Subarea representatives. They took with them the basic plan to work from and their remit was to produce a plan for the completed map of the port. For this work on the Tn side the Port Construction and Repair Groups and Port

Operating Groups were utilised and representatives of 21 Army Group kept in closest contact with them in order to make possible the maximum use of facilities and resources at the disposal of 21 Army Group and to ensure that the planning of shipping and the shipping of stores could be modified to conform to the actual situation in each of the ports as they were captured. The port of Dieppe was captured on 2 September and by the 7th ships were being discharged there. By the end of the month a maximum of 7,200 tons per day were being discharged and being cleared by rail and road. The capture of Boulogne and Ostend in the middle and towards the end of the month did not however provide two additional ports immediately as they were both in a much damaged state. All three ports were heavily demolished, blocked and mined, but in many cases demolitions were inexpertly and incompletely executed. The factor that was most important in preventing the ports from opening was the sinking of block ships in the entrance. This was done both at Ostend and Boulogne but was not done successfully at Dieppe. Antwerp was taken by the end of the month but, of course, could not be operated even though it had been taken practically undamaged because the Scheldt was heavily mined and the Germans still occupied the north bank of the river. By the end of this phase the danger that we should not have adequate port facilities to maintain the armies during the winter was averted and it only remained to bring Antwerp into full operation to change the base of operations from the Normandy beach head to the Belgian. This changeover was already taking place during September and in order not to accumulate large quantities of stores unnecessarily in Normandy, the beaches were closed down by the middle of September, which was earlier than really necessary and traffic was concentrated at Arromanches and Caen, the latter particularly because of suitability for rail clearance.

Another element that was a very important factor, leading to the decision to close down the beaches, was that it became essential to transfer all the MT that had been used for clearance from the beaches to the dumps, and to use it on the long L of C right forward into Holland. The closure of the beaches was a reflection of the urgent importance of providing sufficient lift on the long L of C.

The shortage of MT, which has been mentioned above, also had a very direct bearing on the administration and functioning of Tn units. With the advance most of the units had to change their location at least once if not twice and the movement of all these units with their impedimenta produced problems of the greatest complexity. Not one of the Tn units is fully mobile or even nearly so and about 550 lorry and 100 transporter lifts additional to unit transport were required to move Tn units and equipment to the places where they were required to work. The units could not, therefore, be moved about with complete flexibility from place to place and in some cases were not able to get down to their work as quickly as should theoretically have been possible.

The administration of the Tn service had become reasonably simple in the Normandy beach-head period but, when the L of C stretched from Arromanches to Eindhoven with very poor signal communications, the Tn service was extremely difficult to control. As soon as Brussels was taken, Headquarters moved forward to Brussels. DD Tn (Ports) moved with it and it was organised as in the following diagram:

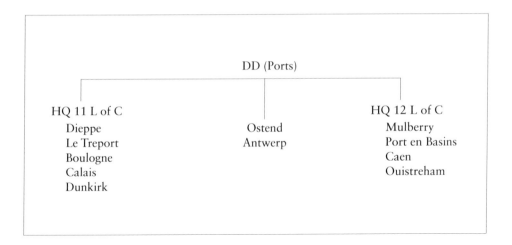

DD (Stores) joined Headquarters at Brussels from the UK and the Railways organisation also was brought forward to Brussels in due course leaving the divisional area organisation at Amiens and Brussels headquarters of the Railway Operating Group still at Caen.

By the end of this phase the Tn service was being planned and reorganised in a form to which it would eventually settle down in the winter to prepare the build-up for the attack on Germany.

PARLIAMENTARY UNDER-SECRETARY OF STATE
FOR DEFENCE FOR THE ARMY

MINISTRY OF DEFENCE

MAIN BUILDING WHITEHALL LONDON SW1A 2HB

Telephone 01-218 2394 (Direct Dialling)

01-218 9000 (Switchboard)

D/US of S(A)/BJH/762

6th December 1979

Dear Nigel,

  I am writing in reply to your letter of 13 November 1979 to Lieutenant Colonel A J Robertson of MS3, which has been passed to me for reply concerning Mrs Sylvia Wild's application for her 1939 - 45 War awards.

  Mrs Wild has now written to my Department giving her former service details and these have been noted by the Army Medal Office. I would be grateful if, when you reply to Mrs Wild, you could forward the enclosed formal acknowledgement of her application together with the envelope containing her Release Book and stamped envelopes, which she forwarded with her letter to MS3. I am afraid that she will have to wait some time before receiving her awards but I think that you will understand that as a result of the Army Medal Office receiving literally hundreds of new applications each month, these must be dealt with in strict chronological order.

  Please assure Mrs Wild that her case will be dealt with as quickly as circumstances permit.

Barney Hayhoe

Sir Nigel Fisher MC MP

SIR NIGEL FISHER MC MP

HOUSE OF COMMONS
LONDON SWIA OAA

10th December, 1979

Dear Mrs. Wild,

      Further to my letter of November 13th,
I have now received the enclosed reply from
the Under Secretary of State for the Army,
returning the papers which you sent to
Col. Robertson. I am sorry for the delay in
sending you the medals, but I do know that this
particular section are very under staffed, indeed,
and have many applications to deal with.

                Yours sincerely,

Mrs. Wild,
110 Brighton Road,
Banstead,
Surrey

JB

MINISTRY OF DEFENCE
Bourne Avenue Hayes Middlesex UB3 1RF

Telephone 081-573 3831 ext

Mrs S P Wild	Your reference
1 Cardinal Drive	
Lisvane	Our reference
South Glamorgan	93/25123/CS(RM)2b/3
CF4 5GD	Date
	10 March 1993

Dear Mrs Wild

In reply to your recent letter, our records show the following particulars of the military service of W/262011 Corporal Sylvia Pamela COOK - Auxiliary Territorial Service:

Enrolled into Auxiliary Territorial Service	14. 5.43
Embodied Same day	
Released to Unemployed List	13.11.46
Discharged	1. 4.54
Cause of Discharge: On termination of engagement	

Service with the Colours: 14. 5.43 to 12.11.46

Overseas service: North West Europe 11. 8.44 to 11.11.45

Military Conduct: Exemplary

Medals issued etc: 1939/45 Star, France and Germany Star, War Medal 1939/45

It would seem that the Army Medal Office got mixed up with the dates as it would appear that you went to the UK, on compassionate leave, on 3 March 1945. Unfortunately the date you returned to NW Europe is not recorded.

I hope this is helpful.

Yours sincerely

K. Welbourne (Mrs.)

K WELBOURNE
for Departmental Record Officer

Recycled Paper

The War Office granted me compassionate leave due to the situation at home in London. I was away just two or three days before being flown back to Brussels. My medals were not 'replacements'; it just took until 1993 to find them!

SIR NIGEL FISHER MC MP

HOUSE OF COMMONS
LONDON SW1A 0AA

13th November, 1979

Dear Mrs. Wild,

      I am sorry I have been rather
a long time in replying to your letter
of October 24th but I had some difficulty
in obtaining information as to who you should
apply to for your medals. I have now heard
that you should write direct to Lt. Col. A.
T. Robertson (Retd) DAMS(A) MS3, Government
Buildings, Stanmore, Middlesex HA7 4PZ, who
will, I think, be able to replace the medals.
I have written to him direct to say that you
will be in touch with him shortly giving
him details of the missing medals.

Yours sincerely,

Mrs. Wild,
110 Brighton Road,
Banstead,
Surrey

TO ALL MEMBERS OF THE
BRITISH FORCES IN GERMANY

Great progress has been made in the de-Nazification of the British Zone and in removing Nazis from all responsibility in German life. Further, the Germans have shown themselves willing to obey my orders and to co-operate in the reconstruction of their country on non-Nazi lines.

I have already modified my orders about non-fraternisation and allowed you to speak and play with little children. I now consider it desirable and timely to permit a further modification of these rules. You may now engage in conversation with adult Germans in the streets and in public places.

You will not for the present enter the homes and houses of the Germans nor permit them to enter any of the premises you are using except for duty or work.

I know the non-fraternisation policy has been a strain upon many of you who have to live and work in close contact with Germans, and I appreciate the loyal way in which you have honoured it.

B. L. Montgomery

Field Marshal,
Commander-in-Chief,
British Zone.

14 July 45.

All Muck, Now Medals

Joan Mant

978 1 84868 259 7

264 pages

Available from all good bookshops or order direct
from our website www.amberleybooks.com

ALSO AVAILABLE FROM AMBERLEY PUBLISHING

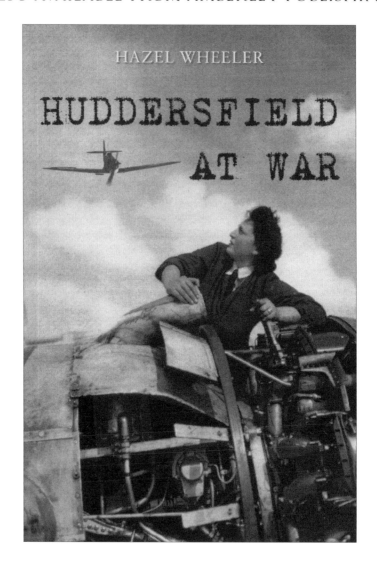

Huddersfield At War
Hazel Wheeler

978 1 84868 408 9
256 pages

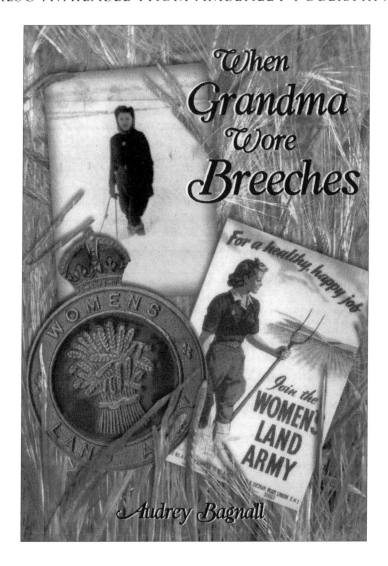

When Grandma Wore Breeches

Audrey Bagnall

978 1 84868 235 1

156 pages

ALSO AVAILABLE FROM AMBERLEY PUBLISHING

A Child's War

The German Occupation of Guernsey as seen through young eyes ...

Molly Bihet

A Child's War

Molly Bihet

978 1 84868 205 4

96 pages

Available from all good bookshops or order direct
from our website www.amberleybooks.com